Complete
iPad for Seniors

Welcome to the only iPad guide book you will ever need!

Using any new technology for the first time can be a little daunting, and with the vast array of features offered by the iPad, confusion can quickly set in too. Worry not though, because we are here to answer all of your questions! We don't just want you to fully understand your new tablet computer, we want you to enjoy using it as much as we do, and with this book to help you we aim to do just that. Whether you use your iPad and iPad mini for work, recreation or organising your social life, you'll want to get the best out of it, and we are here to help you. Within the pages of this publication you will find in-depth expert guides on every feature of the hardware, as well as detailed but always accessible and up-to-date tutorials and reviews to help you get the most out of your iPad and the iOS software at its heart. It's our aim to provide you with accurate and helpful answers to all the questions you have about your Apple iPad.

Contents
Complete iPad for Seniors

Contents

BDM's Senior Series
Complete iPad for Seniors
Volume Eight ISSN 2050-1129

Published by: Black Dog Media Limited (BDM)
Editor: James Gale
Art Director & Production: Mark Ayshford
Production Manager: Karl Linstead
Design: Martin Smith, Sim Dagger
Editorial: Miles Guttery, Russ Ware
Printed and bound in Great Britain by:
Pearl Print Management Limited
Newsstand distribution by:
Comag, Tavistock Road, West Drayton, Middlesex
UB7 7BQ United Kingdom (+44 1895 433600)

International distribution by:
Pineapple Media Limited   www.pineapple-media.com
Copyright © 2014 Black Dog Media

Getting Started with Your iPad

Faster, sleeker and smoother, the iPad is better than ever before! In the following section we will introduce you to the key features of your new iPad and take you through the early stages of its use. With our help you will soon get to grips with your iPad and the amazing iOS 7 software that lurks beneath that beautiful Retina screen.

CONTENTS...

First-Time Set-Up Guide

The quick and easy PC Free option does exactly what you would imagine and removes the need for a PC and iTunes when it comes to activating and syncing your iPad.

PC Free Set Up and Sync

The quick and easy PC Free option does exactly what you would imagine and completely removes the need for a PC and iTunes when it comes to activating and syncing your iPad. The only requirements are a Wi-Fi connection and your hardware, by following our guide you will be quite literally ready to go...

VoiceOver Options

When you first boot up your new iPad you will be greeted by a voice over which will narrate your iPad's actions. You can turn this off by triple clicking the home button.

Step 1 — Power up Your device

When you first power up your new device you will be greeted with the following screen, to move on simply move the lower slider bar to the right.

Hello

Step 2 — Choose Your language

Now you will find yourself on the welcome screen, where you will be asked to select the language that will be used to display all information and menus. Scroll up and down to find your choice and then tap it to select.

Step 3 — Choose Your country

From this screen you will be asked to choose your Country or Region by tapping your choice and you will then move on to the next screen.

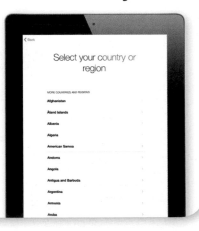

Select your country or region

Step 4 — Choose a Wi-Fi Network

This next screen is fundamental to your progress as you will be asked to connect to a Wi-Fi network. To do this you will need to know your Wi-Fi network password without which you cannot progress.

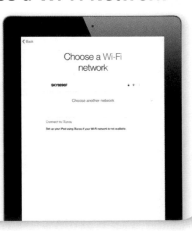

Choose a Wi-Fi network

Step 5 — *Connecting to Wi-Fi*

Now enter your Wi-Fi password and then tap the Join option to link your iDevice to your Wi-Fi network. Having joined your Wi-Fi network, you will automatically activate your iDevice.

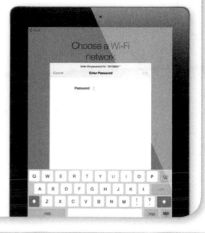

Step 6 — *Using Location Services*

The next screen you see asks you to confirm if you wish to use location services, such as Maps etc. Choose your preferred option to proceed.

Step 7

Having activated your hardware you are now given three different options. Each will set up your iPad in a different manner. Your options are as follows:

"Set Up as new iPad" – Click this option if this is your first iPad and you haven't got an existing Apple ID. By selection this option you will be taken directly to the Apple ID sign-up page where you will need to fill in a brief form and agree to Apple's Terms and Conditions.

"Restore from iCloud Backup" – This option will restore your device to the last point you backed up your information via iCloud. After selecting this option you will be asked to enter your Apple ID and password and then all backed up content from your account will be restored to your new hardware.

"Restore from iTunes" – This option will restore your device to the last point you backed up your information via iTunes. By selecting this option you will end the PC Free set up and be required to link your iPad to your PC via the supplied USB cable.

Having selected the appropriate option now simply tap the next link in the top right.

Step 8 — *Terms & Conditions*

Before you can complete the set-up process and ultimately use your iPad you will need to read and then agree to Apple's Terms and Conditions, you will need to do so before you can move on.

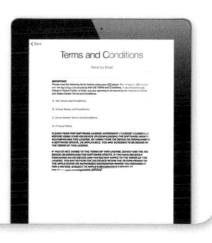

Step 9 — *Activating iCloud*

You are now asked to activate iCloud by moving the smaller slider at the bottom of the screen to the "On" position. We would advise you to do so, as with this option activated you can store contacts, calendars, photos, music, documents, books and apps. This information and any files will be uploaded to your iCloud account and can be accessed from all linked iDevices. To move to the next stage tap "Use iCloud" link at the top-right of the screen.

Step 10 | *Activating Find My iPad*

On this screen you are asked to activate the Find My iPad feature, we would suggest you do this by using the slider at the bottom as this completely free service could prove very useful in locating a lost or stolen iDevice. To move on press the "Use Find My iPad" link.

Step 11 | *iMessage and FaceTime*

During this stage of the set-up process you will be asked to confirm that your linked details from your Apple ID can be used to contact you. It will also enable you to contact others using the iMessage and FaceTime features.

Step 12 | *Enter a Passcode*

Next you will be asked to enter a four digit passcode. You will be required to enter this passcode each time you use your iPhone so ensure it is memorable. You can always skip this step and set up a passcode at a later time when you have thought of a suitable code, the choice is yours.

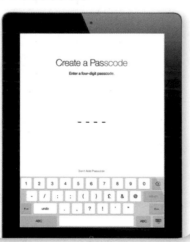

Step 13 | *Set Up Siri*

This next step enables you to access the numerous services provided by Apple's voice activated personal assistant Siri. Tap the option you would like to use, although we would strongly advise you to "Use Siri" a lot!

Step 14 | *Send Data to Apple?*

From here you can choose to provide Apple anonymous diagnostic and usage data, click the preferred option to move on.

Step 15 | *Completing Set-up*

This screen indicates that your PC Free set-up is now complete and you can use your new/re-installed* device.

*You can also use the PC Free set-up installation on any compatible iDevice if you have previously erased all content and settings. This is via the Reset menu from the General options in the Settings App.

Alternative iPad Set-Up Using iTunes

Unlike the previous set up option, for this one you'll need either a Mac running at least OS X 10.5.8 or a PC running Windows 8, 7, Vista or XP (with Service Pack 3). You'll also need to install iTunes 10.5 or a later version and set up an account. This section will take you through a few basic steps to get your iPad up and running if your device is not connected to a Wi-Fi connection.

Step 1 — Syncing to iTunes

The first thing you need to do is connect up your new iPad with your computer. To do this, open iTunes and connect the iPad to your computer using the USB cable that came with it. You can now follow the set up procedure detailed on the previous pages, skipping the Wi-Fi connection section. You can now link your iPad directly to your computer to do the rest.

Step 2 — Syncing Options

You will automatically be taken through the set-up process step by step. Choose whether you want your iPad to automatically sync your music, videos, contacts, calendar, bookmarks and so on every time it's connected to the computer. Alternatively you can choose to sync things manually, it's entirely up to you.

Step 3 — Turn off Auto-Sync

If you want to turn off automatic syncing at a later time, click on Preferences in the iTunes menu, then select devices and check the box where it says 'Prevent iPods, iPhones and iPads from syncing automatically' (Mac). If you're using iTunes on a PC you'll need to go to Edit then Preferences from the iTunes menu.

Step 4 — Set Your Preferences

Regardless of how your preferences are Set-Up you can prevent automatic syncing when you connect your iPad by holding down the command and option keys on Mac or the shift and control keys on PC. Your iPad is now ready to use and you can add a Wi-Fi network when you are in range of one at anytime as detailed in the next section.

The iPad: Inside and Out

With its 64-Bit A7 processor, beautiful high definition Retina screen and powerful front and rear cameras, Apple's latest generation of iPads, the iPad Air and iPad Mini with Retina display, are easily the best tablets money can buy. In this guide we'll look at the iPad's inputs and connections and teach you all you need to know about this amazing hardware.

FaceTime Camera

The design

With the incredibly impressive Retina screen and the added speed and processing power of Apple's A7 chip, you would be forgiven if you thought that the new iPad's aesthetic appeal would suffer! Thankfully the latest generation model retains the visual gloss one would expect from the "coolest" tablet on the face of the planet.

The display

Because the high definition Retina screen plays such a key role in the appeal and the success of the third and now fourth generations of Apple's iPad range, you would expect some serious features here, and Apple hasn't failed us. Offering a jaw-dropping 3.1 million pixels, this is the cleanest, most crisp and detailed display on any tablet currently available. Now you can enjoy HD movies and images in the rich clarity you would expect from a high end desktop computer but in the palm of your hand. The word 'beautiful' doesn't do it justice.

Oleophobic coating?
You don't want to get mired down in the chemistry of this, so to put it simply the glass Apple uses for the new iPad is coated with a polymer to which the oil from human skin does not adhere very well. The result? A shiny, clean and easily viewable 2048-by-1536 resolution screen.

Home Button

The connectivity

Want your online browsing and communication to be secure and fast? Well look no further! Both the Wi-Fi only and the Wi-Fi + 4G LTE versions of the iPad with Retina screen can connect to the Internet using superbly fast 802.11 wireless when in range of a wireless network. The 4G LTE version can also connect via the 4G network at speeds of up to 42 mbps. The new iPad's 802.11 wireless is very fast and is compatible with all major Wi-Fi providers.

The battery

Undeniably one of the most important features for any mobile device, the battery life on the iPad with Retina screen is very impressive, considering the numerous enhancements of this new fourth generation model. There are no other rival products that can hope to match the iPad's 10 hours of life without upgrading the battery pack. Take the power with you in more ways than one.

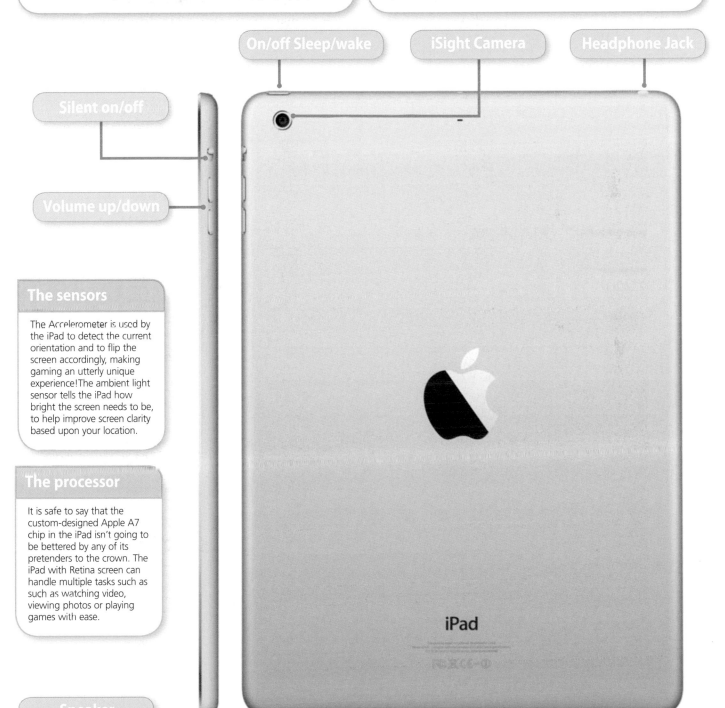

On/off Sleep/wake

iSight Camera

Headphone Jack

Silent on/off

Volume up/down

The sensors

The Accelerometer is used by the iPad to detect the current orientation and to flip the screen accordingly, making gaming an utterly unique experience! The ambient light sensor tells the iPad how bright the screen needs to be, to help improve screen clarity based upon your location.

The processor

It is safe to say that the custom-designed Apple A7 chip in the iPad isn't going to be bettered by any of its pretenders to the crown. The iPad with Retina screen can handle multiple tasks such as such as watching video, viewing photos or playing games with ease.

Speaker

iPad

Using Your iPad's Touchscreen

Although the sizes of the screens on the iPad tablet range do vary, the way you interact with the iPad mini and the iPad with Retina display remains the same. There is much more to using a capacitive, multi-touch screen than you might at first think, and it certainly isn't just about tapping and dragging. Once you master the touchscreen controls, using your iPad becomes a lot easier and quicker.

Touchscreen Actions

Taking you through the various ways you will be able to interact with your iPad's touchscreen.

Touch

The touchscreen is sensitive to the tiny electrical charge in our bodies. This means you only have to tap the screen, not bang down hard with your finger. To activate items on the screen such as application and settings icons, to type letters and symbols using the onscreen keyboard, or to press onscreen buttons, you simply (gently) touch them with your finger.

Touch and hold

Touch and hold is useful in a number of different situations. You can touch and hold an item on the screen by touching it and not lifting your finger until an action occurs. This could be a menu opening, allowing you to customise the Home screen or an icon lifting off the screen and showing that it is able to be moved.

Rotate the screen

On most apps running on the iPad, the orientation of the screen rotates with the tablet as you turn it from portrait to landscape and back again. You can turn this feature on and off in Settings > General > Use Side Switch or by double tapping the home button, swiping to the right and tapping the icon on the far left.

Drag

One of the best things about the iPad is the ability to customise the home screen. To drag items around the screen, touch and hold an item for a moment and then, without lifting your finger, move your finger across the screen until you reach the required position. Lift your finger off the screen and the item will drop into that location (if the location is free). You can drag one item on top of another to create a folder which can then add more items.

Swipe or scroll

Many of the menus or web pages that you can access on the iPad require you to scroll. To swipe or slide, quickly move your finger across the surface of the screen, without pausing when you first touch it. For example, the main Photo app lets you slide the screen left to right to scroll through your pics, and in some Calendar views you swipe quickly across the screen to change the range of time visible.

Double-tap

There are several places where a double-tap results in an action. Tap quickly twice on a webpage, map, or other screen to zoom. You can double-tap a section of a webpage in the Browser to zoom that section to fit the width of the screen. Double-tapping after pinching to zoom in some applications, such as the Browser, reflows a column of text to fit the width of the screen.

Pinch to Zoom

In some applications (such as Maps, Browser, and Gallery), you can zoom in and out by placing two fingers on the screen at once and pinching them together (to zoom out) or spreading them apart (to zoom in). This also works to zoom in and out in the Camera app.

Your iPad
Accessibility Guide

Many new electronic devices now offer a range of accessibility features for users with visual, hearing or other disabilities. The iPad, along with iOS 7, contains not only the usual options for increasing text size or changing the contrast of the screen, but also includes an innovative voice-over feature, subtitles and captions, and much more. Here's how to make the iPad accessible to almost anyone.

Vision Accessibility Options

VoiceOver

VoiceOver actually changes the way you control your iPad, making it possible for someone with little or no sight to navigate around the device with greater accuracy. For example, touch or drag your finger around the screen and VoiceOver tells you what's there. Tap a button to hear a description of what is selected, or double-tap to activate that app or function. Swipe up or down to adjust a slider. Flick left and right to move from one app to the next. When you interact with an element on the screen, a black rectangle appears around it, so sighted users can follow along.

When you prefer privacy, you can activate a screen curtain to turn off the display so no one can see it, even as you're controlling it. And when VoiceOver is talking, the volume of any background audio from music or video automatically lowers, "ducking" under the voice, so you can hear VoiceOver clearly.

Because VoiceOver is integrated in iOS, it works with all the built-in apps, including Safari, Mail, App Store, iTunes, Music, Calendar, Reminders and Notes. You can also create custom labels for buttons in any app, including third-party apps.

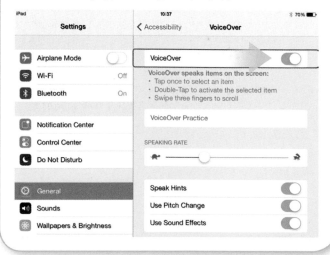

Zoom

Zoom, as the name suggests, allows you to magnify anything on the iPad screen. Turn this feature on and the display will automatically zoom in. You can then control the zoom level by tapping anywhere on screen with three fingers. If you need to move the screen around to see areas which are now out of sight because of the zoom level, you simply drag the screen using the three-finger touch. To change the level of zoom, double-tap with three fingers and then drag them over the screen on the second tap. A simple double tap with three fingers instantly zooms in 200 per cent, but you can adjust the magnification between 100 and 500 per cent.

Quite aside from its accessibility use, Zoom is useful for anyone to have on if they read a lot of text on the iPad. Being able to quickly zoom the screen can be handy, and unless you are using other accessibility features (which sometimes also use the three-finger tap), it is unlikely that you will accidentally turn zoom on when you don't need it.

Invert Colours

Inverting the colours on the iPad changes the display to something like the night mode found on many e-reader apps. By switching the light areas (usually background) to dark, and the text to white, users with vision problems may find it easier and less of a strain to see and read. It does, however, make some screens look slightly strange (including the home screen).

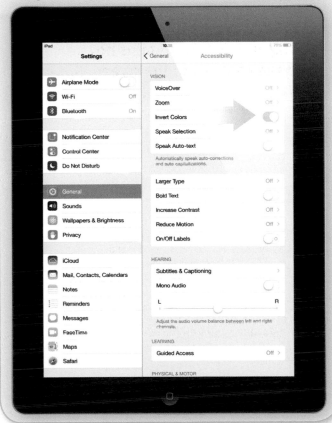

Bold Text

Bold Text is a system-wide change which makes all of the text on the device bolder and easier to read. When you apply this feature, the iPad will need to restart before the change is able to be seen.

Applying the Bold Text feature will not make a huge difference, but it will make menu text, etc., easier to read in most cases.

Speak Selection

In a similar way to VoiceOver, Speak Selection gives you the option to have some text read aloud to you. The main difference is that speak selection only reads text that is selected or highlighted by the user. This means that it won't speak every menu heading you touch or an icon you tap, but it will read out text you highlight in a Word document, for example. To use speak selection, activate it in the settings and then open the document, note or website you want to have spoken. Highlight a section of text as you would normally, and then tap Speak from the action menu that appears.

You can change the language and the accent of the voice that Speak Selection uses in the Accessibility Settings. You can also choose the have the words highlighted as they are read out, to give you a easy visual clue to the progress of the audio.

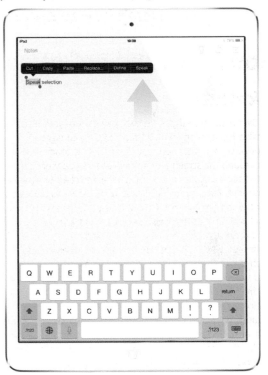

Speak Auto-text

Used on its own or in conjunction with Speak Selection, Speak Auto-text will automatically speak aloud and auto-corrections and auto-capitalisations in the text documents, notes or emails you compose.

Larger Type

With Larger Dynamic Type enabled, any app which supports the feature will automatically adjust the font size to the level you select in the Accessibility Settings. As you adjust the size slider in the settings, the text on that page will increase or decrease in size to show you the change you can expect to see.

Apps which support Larger Dynamic Type include Mail, Safari, iBooks, Notes, Reminders, Keynote, Numbers, Pages and the Calendar. You may find that some third-party apps do not support this feature, but many of the most popular and better-known apps do.

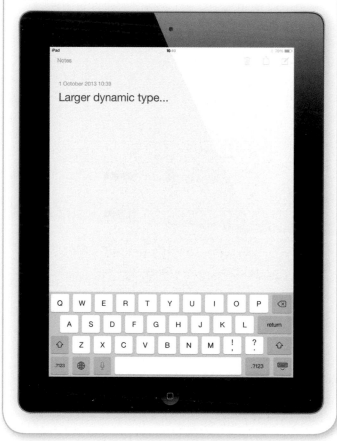

More Vision Settings

Increase Contrast
This will improve the contrast on some backgrounds to increase legibility.

Reduce Motion
This will reduce the motion of the user interface, including the parallax effect of icons and alerts.

On/Off Labels
This simply adds a small label to any on/off switch, to make it easier to check if a setting is enabled.

Hearing Accessibility Options

Subtitles & Captioning

This feature applies closed captioning or subtitles for the deaf or hard of hearing on any video or streaming media content that supports it. You can choose the style of the subtitles in the Accessibility Settings menu to suit your preference, or you can create your own style. This allows you to alter text size, font, text colour, opacity and several other settings. You can check how the style looks by tapping the arrow icon at the top corner of the image on the settings page.

Mono Audio

This allows you to change the audio output of the iPad to mono rather than stereo. Useful for evening up sound if you are hard of hearing in one ear only. Depending on which ear you have difficulties with, you can change which channel the audio comes from using the slider below the switch on the Accessibility Settings page.

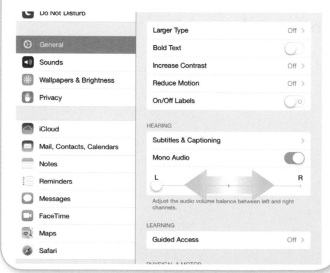

Guided Access

Guided Access helps you to stay focused on a task while using your iPhone, iPad or iPod touch. Guided Access limits your device to a single app and lets you control which app features are available. You can Use Guided Access to temporarily restrict your iOS device to a particular app, disable areas of the screen that aren't relevant to a task, or areas where an accidental gesture might cause a distraction and even disable the hardware buttons.

To enable Guided Access, tap Settings > General > Accessibility > Guided Access. From there you can turn Guided Access on or off, set a passcode that controls the use of Guided Access and prevents someone from leaving an active session, and set whether the device can go to sleep during a session. To start a Guided Access session, open the app you want to run, triple-click the Home button and adjust settings for the session, then click Start.

AssistiveTouch

AssistiveTouch helps you use your iPhone, iPad, or iPod touch if you have difficulty touching the screen or pressing the buttons. You can use AssistiveTouch to perform gestures that are difficult for you. You can also use a compatible adaptive accessory (such as a joystick) together with AssistiveTouch to control your iOS device.

To enable AssistiveTouch on your device, tap Settings > General > Accessibility > AssistiveTouch.

Enable Triple-click Home (three consecutive Home button presses) to quickly toggle AssistiveTouch on or off by tapping Settings > General > Accessibility > Triple-click Home. If you need to adjust the speed required to activate Double and Triple-click Home you can go to Settings > General > Accessibility > Home-click Speed.

Home-click Speed

A lot of the accessibility features require you to activate them using the triple-click home method. This can sometimes be difficult to perform properly, particularly if you have a disability which affects the hands and fingers. You can, however, change the speed that the button needs to be pressed using this option. You can choose from default, slow and slowest.

Accessibility Shortcut

If you have several accessibility options enabled, you may need to choose which of them is activated when you triple-click the home button. Not all of the accessibility settings require triple-click, but VoiceOver, Invert Colours, Zoom, Switch Control and AssistiveTouch all do. Simply tap the Accessibility Shortcut option and choose the feature you want to be able to control using triple-click home. All of the other features can still be used, but they will need to be controlled using the main settings rather than a shortcut.

Getting more from Your iPad

In this jargon-free section we are going to introduce and then take you through all of the key apps and features of the new iPad. We'll show you how to get the best out of such fantastic tools as the voice-controlled Siri, the powerful Safari Internet browser, the 3D-enhanced Maps and much, much more.

CONTENTS...

How to use the Control Center

As its name suggests the Control Center places you in quick and easy control of the central functionality of the iPad. Having accessed this shortcut menu you will be one screen tap away from accessing key applications or adjusting core settings, these shortcuts will leave you in total control of your device.

Accessing the Control Center

To open the Control Center whether if you are on the home screen or using any app simply swipe from the home button to the upper area of the iPad's screen and this new menu will appear.

Airplane Mode

By tapping this icon you will switch on Airplane Mode. This mode switches off all of your iPad's access to incoming signals such as 4G, Wi-Fi etc., which could cause issues with the aircraft's instruments while you are flying. To turn off Airplane mode, when you are back on terra firma simply open the Control Center and tap this icon for a second time.

Wi-Fi

You may wish to turn off your links to your Wi-Fi connection or those around you when you are out and about, if you are accessing mobile data or wish to limit web access if you are sharing your iPad with a second party. To switch off all Wi-Fi connections to your iPad simply tap this icon on the Control Center, to re-activate Wi-Fi it tap it once again.

Bluetooth

Many accessories, or on some occasions, applications will require linked access to your iPad via Bluetooth. Pairing a device using a Bluetooth connection is a quick and easy way to link your iPad to another device without the need for Wi-Fi or mobile data, to switch on your Bluetooth signal tap this icon, once again to disable it repeat the process.

Do Not Disturb

If you have set up your Do Not Disturb preferences, you can instantly switch on this mode via the Control Center by tapping this icon. Remember, if you have this mode switched on you will not receive calls or messages so ensure you use this quick link on the Control Center when needed.

Screen Orientation Lock

Upon occasions you will want to lock your iPad in either landscape (Sideways) or portrait (Upright). Be it browsing the Internet in landscape mode or taking a photograph in portrait mode you don't want the iPad to switch to the opposite view on its own. To avoid this simply tap this icon while holding your device in the position you wish.

Brightness

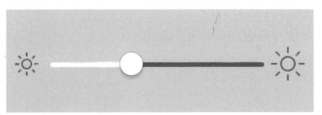

Although the Auto Brightness option that comes as standard with the iPad will almost always find the perfect screen setting based upon the light sources that surround you, there may come a time, particularly when you are in bright sunlight where you may wish to tweak the brightness settings yourself, and using this slider you can do just that.

Music/Podcast Controls

If we were to pick one feature of the Control Center we have used more than any of the others it has to be this. With a swipe of the screen, followed by a single tap you can instantly return to listening to your favourite podcast or latest iTunes purchase. You can also adjust the volume, or skip to the next track all from the Control Center, which is sweet music to all.

Timer

The Control Center offers you a quick link to one of the most useful features of the Clock app, the Timer mode. By tapping this icon you will instantly open this application on its Timer setting. The uses for this mode are many from boiling an egg to a learning aid making it a fine inclusion.

Camera

The countless excellent features of the iPad's camera are covered in this guide so you won't need any further motivation to make use of the iPad's amazing camera. If your iPad is on the lock screen you can access the camera by swiping upward, when your iPad is in use you can access the camera via this shortcut link.

How to use the Clock App

Among the most impressive elements of the iOS 7 update are the hundreds of smaller improvements. One such small, but very useful, improvement is the new Clock app.

Using the World Clock Made Easy

Step 1 By default, the world clock shows the time in several cities, including Cupertino (the home of Apple). You can either add your own time zones to the existing ones, or remove them and start from scratch.

Step 2 To add a city to those already shown, tap the clock with the + in the middle of the face. An A-Z list will pop-up, allowing you to choose the city you want to add. You can also search for cities.

Step 3 If you want to remove the existing cities, tap the Edit button in the top-left corner, then tap the minus button next to the those you want to remove. Tap Delete to confirm the action.

Step 4 On the large world map below the clock faces, you will see the locations of the cities you add. The time is shown on the map, as well as the temperature and current weather conditions.

How do you use The Stopwatch Feature?

The stopwatch feature works exactly as you might expect. There is a start button to start the timer, which changes to a Lap button when the clock is counting. Each time you tap the Lap button, the lap time is displayed below the main stopwatch readout (which continues to count up). Simply tap the red Stop button to stop the stopwatch and then tap again to reset it to 00:00.0.

Setting Alarms

Step 1 Tap the Alarm tab at the bottom of the clock screen to start editing your alarms. To set a new alarm, tap the + button at the top-right of the screen. This opens a Add Alarm window.

Step 2 Use the two wheels to pick a time for the alarm to sound. You can also choose which days the alarm will play, the alarm sound you want, whether the alarm can be snoozed and what the alarm is called.

Step 3 Your new alarm will be displayed at the top of the screen, as well as on the 24-hour display below. If you have more than one alarm set up, you can select each on this 24-hour display.

Step 4 You can also alter the time and day the alarm will sound by touching and holding it on the 24-hour display. You can then drag the alarm to whatever time and day you want.

Step 5 You can turn each alarm on or off independently by highlighting it and tapping the on/off button. To remove or edit an alarm, tap Edit and either tap the time you want to change or tap the minus button to delete.

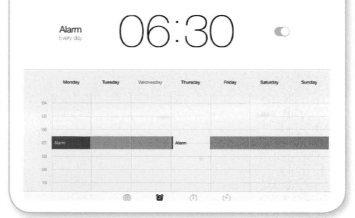

Using The Timer Feature

The Timer app can be set to count down from up to 23 hrs and 59 mins. When it reaches zero an alarm will sound. The current alarm sound is shown below the timer display. You can choose another alarm sound by clicking the Sounds button in the top-left corner. There are a number of preset alarm sounds to choose from, as well as the option to buy alarm tones from iTunes. You can test any of the sounds available by tapping its name in the list.

How to use the Messages App

iMessage is one of the most amazing features of iOS 7, enabling instant group chatting, picture and file sharing, and more.

The Messages App's key features explained

We've highlighted the key features of this application to help you better understand how it works.

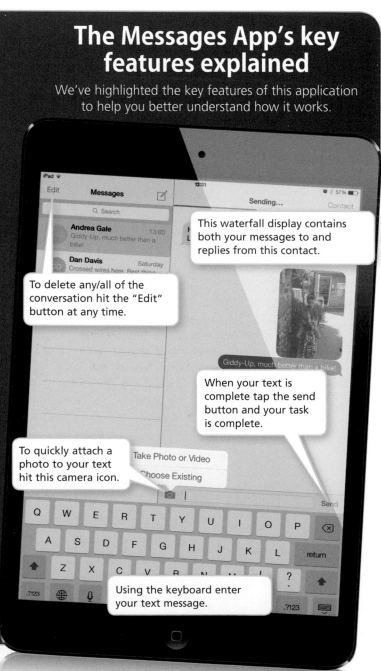

This waterfall display contains both your messages to and replies from this contact.

To delete any/all of the conversation hit the "Edit" button at any time.

When your text is complete tap the send button and your task is complete.

To quickly attach a photo to your text hit this camera icon.

Using the keyboard enter your text message.

Step 1 The first thing you'll need to do is make sure iMessage is turned on. To do this tap the settings icon on your iPad's homescreen. Select iMessage from the list that appears. You may have to scroll down to find it.

Step 2 On the iMessage settings screen you'll see an on/off switch. Slide it to the on position to enable iMessages. Wait a few moments as iMessage initialises. A message should appear to let you know it's in the process of activating.

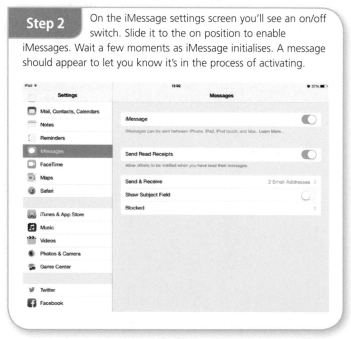

Step 3 After activating iMessage you'll notice various configuration options have become available which enable you to adjust the settings to your liking.

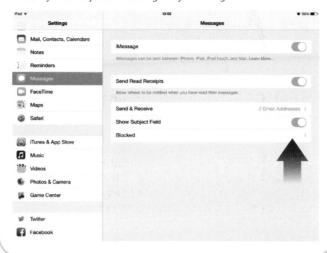

Step 4 Read Receipts are notifications sent out by your device to your contacts to let them know when you've read messages they've sent to you in iMessage. You may not want people to know immediately that you've read their message but thankfully Apple have included the option to turn these notifications off. Turn off Read Receipts if you don't want people to know that you've read their messages. They will still be notified when the message is delivered however. If you're happy for people to receive Read Receipts when you read their messages, turn the option on. Just remember that people will know immediately when you've read their message so remember to reply or they'll think you're ignoring them!

Step 5 Received At is where you set up the devices and accounts through which you want to receive your iMessages. When using an iPad your phone number will automatically be set as your Receive At address. There are more options and the ability to add an email address for people with multiple devices all running iMessages. For example you might want to sync your iPad, iPod touch and iPhone, all with iMessage running on them.

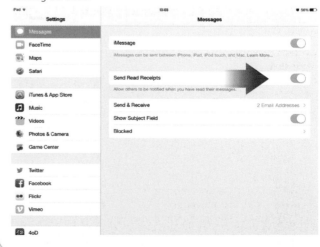

Step 6 To add an email address you'll need an Apple ID. When you attempt to add a new email address you'll be prompted to enter this, then the email address you want to add. Once verified the address will become active.

Step 7 Caller ID enables you to choose which of your selected addresses you want your messages to be sent from. In other words, whichever device or address you're actually using, the one that appears to the person you're messaging will be the one that you select here. This also ensures that all your communications are synced across all your devices.

When all settings are configured to your satisfaction you're ready to get messaging. Return to the home screen by tapping the Home button.

Step 8 Tap the iMessage icon to get started.

Step 9 To Start an iMessage conversation tap the pencil and paper button at the top right of the screen. This brings up the New Message screen.

Step 10 In the To field you need to type the number or email address of the person you want to message. If the number or address isn't registered for iMessage the contact will turn green which tells you that the message will be sent as a text message. iMessages can only be sent to other iOS 7 devices.

Step 11 When you enter a contact who's using iMessage the Send button will change to blue which lets you know your message is being sent via iMessage. Type in your message and when you're done, tap Send.

Step 12 The delivery status icon lets you know when your message has been sent. If the recipient of the message has Read Receipts turned on then this will change to Read once they've looked at the message.

Step 13 You can see when the other person is typing as three dots in a speech bubble appear in the bottom left of the message field.

Step 14 You can add photos to your messages by tapping the camera icon to the left of the message text field.

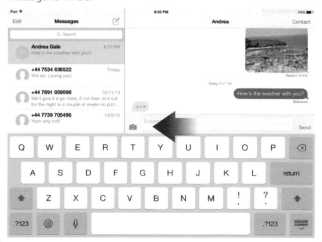

Step 15 You can add multiple recipients. When group messaging, the name of the sender appears above each message so you can easily keep track of who said what.

Step 16 If you receive messages through iMessage when you're not in iMessage itself they'll appear as standard iOS 7 notifications. Just tap on the message notification to go straight to the conversation screen and reply.

How to use the Contacts App

The iPad includes advanced address book functionality that will enable you to keep all your important contact details organised and easily accessible.

The Contacts App's key features explained

We've highlighted the key features of this application to help you understand better how it works.

Search for a specific contact, email or number via this search engine link.

Tap the "+" icon to enter the details of a new contact.

A contact's full details can be viewed and edited via this window.

Your complete contacts listings for a specific letter are displayed here.

Skip directly to a contact by clicking the corresponding first letter of their surname.

How do I start Adding Contacts to my Address Book?

Step 1 To manually add a contact open Contacts and tap the 'plus' button. You can then add all their basic information including phone number, email, website and address.

Step 2 If you want to add additional information click the Add Field button for more options.

Step 3 You can also sync your Google and Yahoo! contacts through iTunes. If you have a MobileMe or Microsoft Exchange account, you can enable contacts to add them automatically.

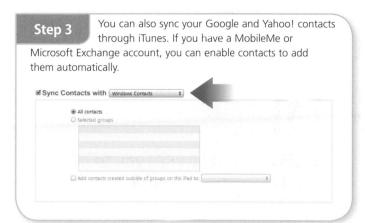

Step 4 To search for a contact enter the name in the search field at the top of the screen.

What if I have the same person on several Contact Lists?

You can 'unify' contacts that appear multiple times in your synced accounts by opening one of their profiles and tapping the person-plus button then selecting their other profile. Repeat this process for all the person's profiles and all their details will then appear in one entry.

More Contacts Options

Creating a Favourites List:
You can create a Favourites list for FaceTime contacts. Just open their contact details and tap Favourites.

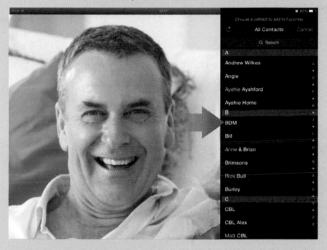

Deleting/Editing Contacts:
To delete or edit any contact open the profile and tap edit.

Sharing Contacts with others:
You can also email contacts to other people by simply tapping the Share Contact option.

Sharing Contact details via Text

Should you wish to send the contact details from your list to another iPad or compatible smartphone user, use our brief tutorial as your guide.

Step 1 From your Contacts app select the details you wish to share and tap the "Share Contact" button on the lower left.

Step 2 By doing this you will bring up the Sharing options tab. Select the format you wish to send the details (We are using SMS although the basics remain the same for Email) and proceed.

Step 3 You will now see the contact details as an attachment. Enter any text you wish and then tap "Send" to complete the process.

Note: Should you receive a contact simply tap the attachment to add it to your existing contacts list.

Can I add Pictures to my Contacts?

Step 1 You may if you wish. Open up a contact and tap edit then select the Add Photo option.

Step 2 Browse to select the appropriate photo and tap Choose.

Keep in Touch with Your Contacts

The main reason for having and maintaining the Contacts app on your iPad is to enable you to keep in touch with your family and friends, and keep track of those important numbers and details that you will want to lay your fingers on quickly. In this section of the guide we will teach you how to get in touch with your contacts with just a few taps of your screen.

Step 1 Open the Contacts app and using the left side pane, scroll down through your contacts until you reach the person you wish to contact.

Step 2 Alternatively you can shortcut the Contacts pane by tapping the search bar at the top of the left pane and entering the contacts details, which will take you directly to it.

Step 3 Having now found the contact you wish to interact with, you will notice there are three options open to you depending how you want to get in touch.

Step 4 To the right of the number(s) you have linked to your contact is the message icon. Tap the speech bubble and enter your message as usual.

Step 5 Below the contact's number(s) you'll find direct links to the FaceTime application. You can select either video or audio call, and this will be placed immediately.

How to use the Notes App

Notes is a very simple app, but incredibly useful. It lets you use your iPad as a notebook, to jot down anything, anywhere, at any time.

The Notes App's key features explained

We've highlighted the key features of this application to help you understand better how it works.

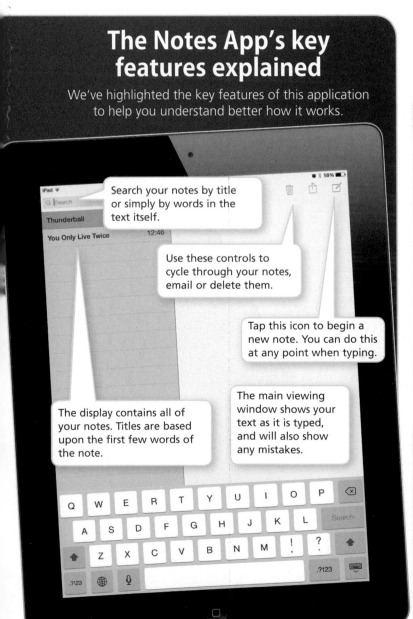

Search your notes by title or simply by words in the text itself.

Use these controls to cycle through your notes, email or delete them.

Tap this icon to begin a new note. You can do this at any point when typing.

The display contains all of your notes. Titles are based upon the first few words of the note.

The main viewing window shows your text as it is typed, and will also show any mistakes.

Using Notes

Notes doesn't just work like a notepad, it looks like one too! Here's how to get the most out of it.

Step 1 Open Notes and tap the 'plus' symbol to add a new note then tap the page to open the keyboard and begin typing. All your existing notes appear as a list on the left of the screen in the order in which they were created with the most recent at the top.

Step 2 Tap a note to read or edit it or scroll through your notes using the arrow buttons. Notice that above the notes list is a text field. Enter keywords in here to quickly search for key words. Finally to delete a note, open it and tap the bin icon.

Using the iPad's Built-in Dictionary

A dictionary is an essential tool whenever you are writing, no matter if you are holding a pen or tapping on your iPad's touchscreen. Luckily the iPad comes with a fantastic built-in dictionary that can be accessed from the majority of apps that use the keyboard. This dictionary also comes with access to numerous languages, so this guide will examine both of these features.

Step 1 When you are inputting your text and require the dictionary for a certain word, press and hold on this word until it is completely highlighted; this will bring up a pop-up menu. Now tap on the Define link to bring up the dictionary option. To select a definition swipe to the right to bring up your choice.

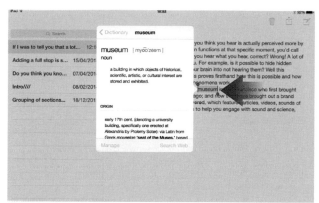

Step 2 You can also download additional dictionaries by tapping the Manage link from the bottom left of the dictionary window. Here you can add various dictionaries from a wide array of different languages and locations by tapping the iCloud link to the right of each one. This new dictionary will download automatically.

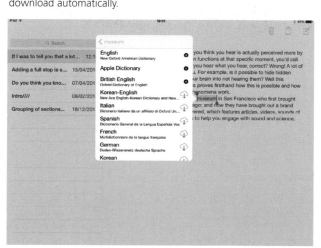

Using Automatic Correction in Notes

Spelling mistakes can cause confusion not only to yourself but even more so to those reading your notes. Although the iPad already has a fantastic dictionary built-in, you can also access the extremely useful Auto-Correction and Check Spelling features to make both your Note and general writing that little bit easier for all users.

Step 1 Open the iPad's Setting app and from the General link, tap on the Keyboard link from the main pane. From this screen make sure that the Auto-Correction and Check Spelling sliders are set the on position, then return to the Notes application and open up. NOTE: These features will also work on other apps.

Step 2 Now when you are typing in the Notes app, or in any other app that requires keyboard input, and you make a mistake with your spelling, the iPad will either automatically correct the spelling or highlight the mistake with a red line. Tap this word and you will bring up suggested replacements.

How to use the Calendar App

Friday 27

With the iPad's Calendar software you never need to miss an appointment again. In fact you can organise your entire life.

The Calendar App's key features explained

We've highlighted the key features of this application to help you understand better how it works.

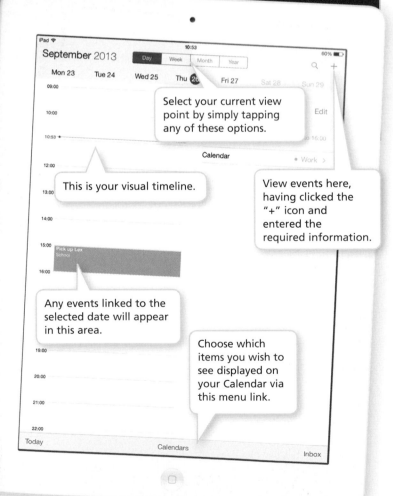

Select your current view point by simply tapping any of these options.

This is your visual timeline.

View events here, having clicked the "+" icon and entered the required information.

Any events linked to the selected date will appear in this area.

Choose which items you wish to see displayed on your Calendar via this menu link.

Exploring the Calendar App

In today's busy world it's important to organise your time effectively. This step-by-step guide will take you through the many uses of the Calendar app and show you how to get the most from it.

Step 1   Tap the Calendar icon to open the application and you will find yourself taken directly to today's page, as always.

By tapping the Calendars icon to the top right you'll bring down a new tab featuring a list of all your synced calendars.

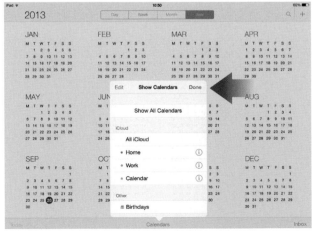

Step 2

To turn different calendars on and off just tap on them. Active calendars have a tick next to them. Tap Done at any time to enter the main calendar view where you'll find events from all active calendars displayed. You can go back and activate or deactivate calendars at any time by tapping the Calendars button to the top left of the screen.

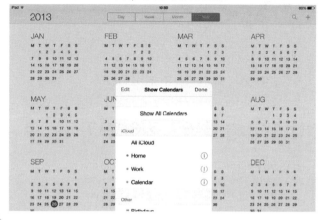

Step 3

To add an event tap the plus symbol to the top right of the screen. Enter a title and location for the event in the field provided, choose a start and end date and time, set whether the event is to repeat either daily, weekly, every two weeks, monthly or yearly and decide whether you want to be alerted in advance.

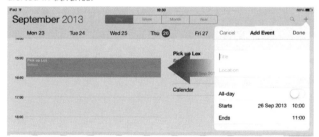

If you choose to receive an alert you can determine how long in advance you want to receive the alert. You can also enter any notes or details in the bottom field. When all details are entered tap Done.

Step 4

To edit an event, tap the event and then tap the Edit button that appears at the top right of the screen. From here you can tap on any of the fields to change the details.

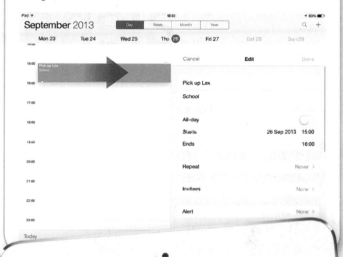

Step 5
To delete an event tap it, tap the Edit button then tap the red Delete Event button at the bottom of the screen.

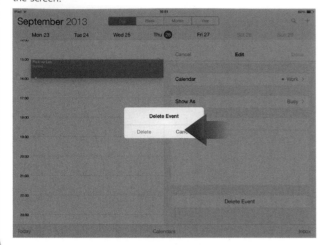

Step 6
To search for specific events tap the search field at the top of the main screen. You can search for titles, locations or keywords that appear in the event description. As you type, matching events will appear automatically enabling you to open the appropriate one without having to type in the whole name or description.

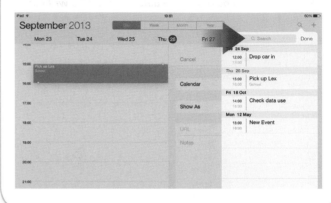

Syncing Calendars with Desktop Apps

While your iPad Calendar application is a fantastic addition to your home screen, you may have previously used other similar applications on your desktop computer, so in this section we will be looking at how you can merge the two.

Step 1
To Sync Calendar on your tablet with other calendars on your computer via iTunes, connect your iPad to your computer and choose iPad Info.

Step 2
To Sync calendars over the air you'll need to turn Calendars on in your Google, Yahoo!, MobileMe or Microsoft Exchange accounts.

Inviting Contacts to an Event

One of the most amazing features of the iPad's Calendar app is that you aren't simply limited to adding an event to your Calendar as a reminder for yourself. You can also remind any number of your friends and family from your Contacts app too. This short guide will teach you how to share dates with others without any fuss at all.

Step 1

Open the Settings app and select iCloud. From these options make sure that the Calendar slider is set to the on position or this guide won't work.

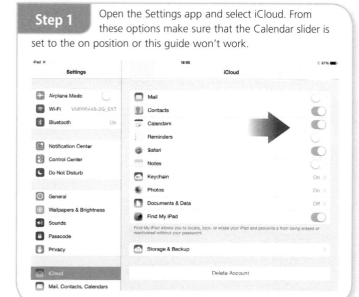

Step 2

Open the Calendar app and tap on the "+" icon on the top right corner and input the information you require about the event using the keyboard.

Step 3

Remember you will be sharing this with others you will need to be quite specific regarding the information you input here for their reference.

Step 4

Now scroll down to the Invitees link and tap on it to bring up a pop up, tap "+" to select your invitees from your contacts then tap done.

Step 5

They will now be sent a message about the event and can confirm they are coming and the event will be added to their Calendar app.

Using the iSight Camera

One of the most popular improvements to the latest generation of iPad is the new five megapixel iSight camera, which is loaded with great features. Smile please!

The iSight Camera's key features explained

We've highlighted the key features of this application to help you understand better how it works.

Tap here to switch between the front and rear mounted cameras.

This is the main viewing window, what you see here will be your photo or video.

Use this slider to switch between the photo and video camera settings.

Tap here to be taken directly to your photo and video collection in the Photos app.

Capturing Still Photographs and Video Explained

For this guide we will take you through using the iPad's 5MP camera to take photographs and video clips. By following this comprehensive step-by-step guide you will be capturing priceless memories within moments.

Step 1 — To Start camera tap the Camera Icon.

Step 2 — To flip between the front and back cameras tap the icon of a camera with arrows around it at the bottom right of the screen.

Step 3   To switch between video and standard camera move the little slider at the bottom right. Left selects standard camera and right selects the video camera.

Step 4   With regular camera selected, tapping anywhere in the view window brings up the zoom control. Slide the slider to the right to zoom in and the left to zoom out.

Step 5   For additional iSight camera features you will need to return to the home screen and into the Setting option. From this link select Camera and from this screen you can switch on the Grid mode, which will place a nine section grid on screen when you shoot photos or videos.

Step 6   To take a photo tap the large button with a camera on it on the right side of the screen.

Step 7 The last picture you took is displayed at the bottom left of the screen. Tap it to see how it came out. To return to the camera view tap Done or tap Camera Roll to go to your photo library.

Step 8 To record a video ensure that the slider selector at the bottom right of the screen is moved to the right. Press the red record button and the camera will start recording video. A timer appears in top right of the screen. The red button will flash to indicate it's recording. Tap the button again to stop recording.

Auto Video Stabilisation

The auto video stabilisation features of the iSight camera doesn't require any input from the user or changes to the Settings.

Step 9 When you stop recording the video appears to the bottom left of the screen. Tap it to view it. You can scrub through using the slider at the top of the screen, delete it by tapping the bin icon or tap the arrow-in-a-box icon to share it.

Importing Photos and Videos to Your iPad

The iPad is a perfect virtual photo album, with which you can share your treasured family memories with all, no matter where you find yourself. But what if you want to share photos that you didn't actually take using your iPad or those devices you share over iCloud? This short tutorial will take you through how to upload/import images from your desktop computer to your iPad.

Step 1   Place the images you wish to share into the My Pictures folder on your desktop computer.

Step 2   Connect your iPad to your computer via the USB cable.

Step 3   Open iTunes and select your iPad from the left column.

Step 4   Now select the Photos option from the upper bar.

Step 5   Select the Sync from My Pictures option and sync your iPad.

Step 6   All compatible photos will now be imported to your iPad allowing you to view them through the Photos app.

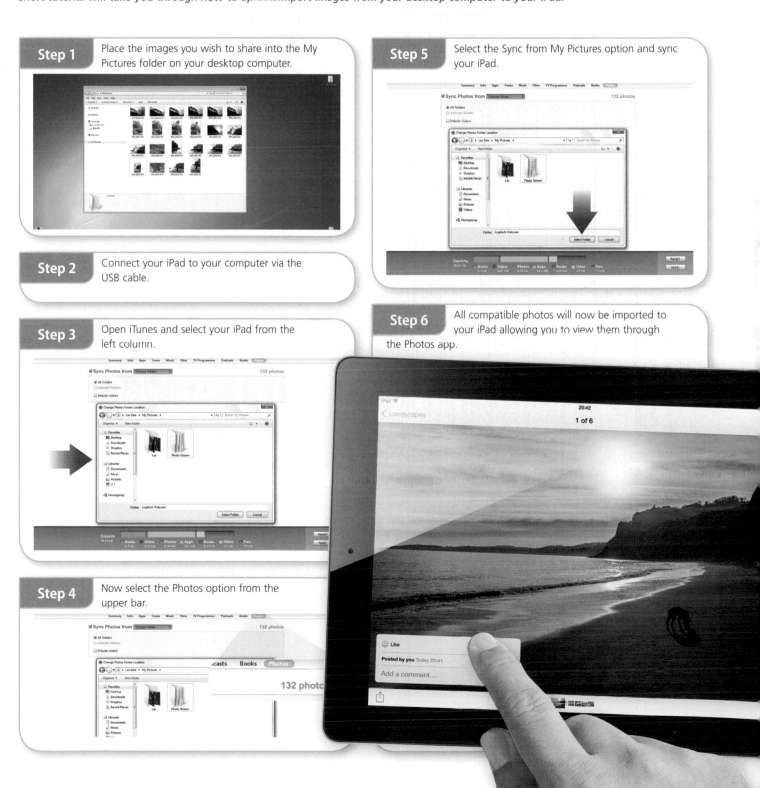

How to use the
Photos App

Here is where you'll find all the photos and videos you've taken as well as images downloaded from the web.

The Photos App's key features explained

We've highlighted the key features of this application to help you understand better how it works.

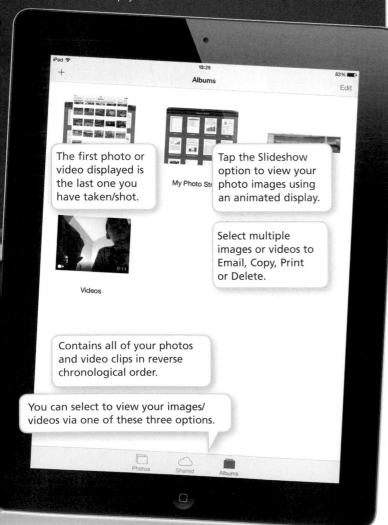

The first photo or video displayed is the last one you have taken/shot.

Tap the Slideshow option to view your photo images using an animated display.

My Photo Str

Select multiple images or videos to Email, Copy, Print or Delete.

Videos

Contains all of your photos and video clips in reverse chronological order.

You can select to view your images/videos via one of these three options.

Photos   Shared   Albums

Using the Photos Application – General Tips

This is where all the photographs and videos you take are stored...

| Step 1 | Tap Photos to open your photo and video library. Then tap any photo or video to view it. |

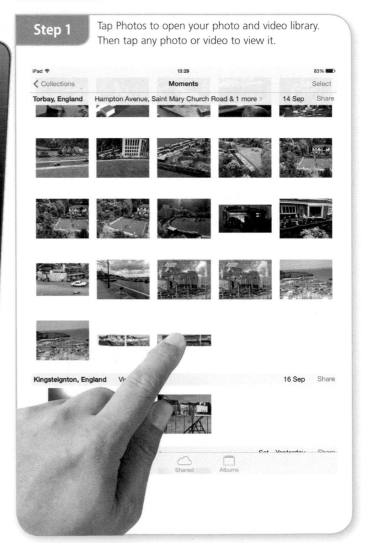

Step 2 To zoom in on a picture just pinch. When zoomed in you can move the picture around by dragging it with your finger.

Step 3 Tap any picture or video to view it, or to go to the next or previous photo or video in your library simply swipe your finger across the screen to the left or right respectively.

Step 4 To delete any photo or video, open it and tap the bin icon.

Step 5 To share any photo or video, open it then tap the arrow-in-a-box button to bring up your sharing options.

Editing Techniques Made Easy

Before the launch of iOS 7 if you wanted to alter your photographs you would need to download an additional application from the App Store. Thankfully Apple has packed this even more awesome version of the iOS with a photo editing suite directly within the Photos app. Here's how to get the most from it.

Step 1
Open the Photos App and select the image you wish to edit from the camera roll.

Step 2
To bring up the key editing tools press the "Edit" button in the upper right corner.

Step 3
Moving from left to right on the bottom bar, the first tool allows you to **rotate** the image through a full 360 degrees in four positions. Simply tap the icon until you have the image in the position you wish.

Step 4
The second icon is the **Auto Enhance** tool which will use the internal software to increase colour levels, brightness and tones to their suggested levels. A second tap will turn off these enhancements.

Step 5
The third option enables you to place visual filters on your photographs, to give them a new and unique look. Simply choose the filter you wish to use from the eight options displayed at the bottom of the screen and then tap Apply.

Step 6
The **Red-Eye** and **Crop** tools round out the options. To use Red-Eye removal tap this option and then tap the effected areas of the photo. Crop enables you to resize a selected area of the image. The "Aspect Ratio" link gives you various pre-set size options which overlay the image. Alternatively drag each corner to resize the grid, or drag the whole grid over the selected area, hit "Crop" and then save the image.

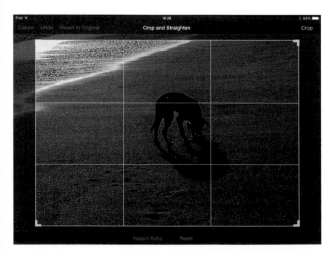

Creating New Albums

On previous versions of the Apple iOS, all images and video clips, whether downloaded or captured via the iPad camera, were stored in one large folder which was accessible through the Photos application. This was one of the few flaws of the iOS as it made locating images very difficult. This flaw has been corrected, and you are now able to organise your images and videos as you wish.

Step 1 To organise your photos into new custom Albums, simply hit the right pointing arrow icon at the upper right of the screen.

Step 2 Select the images you wish to group and tap the "Add to" on the top bar and select "New Album" from the pop-up tab.

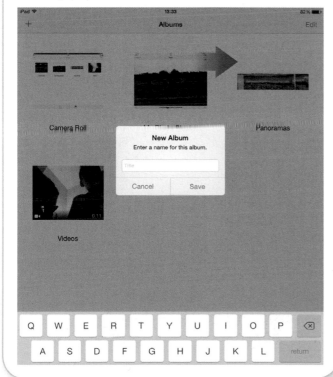

Step 3 Now simply name the new Album and confirm your choice.

Step 4 When you return to your albums you will see your new addition at the bottom of the page.

Using Email on Your iPad

If you are using your iPad for business or personal use, understanding how to get the most from your email app is essential.

Mail, Contacts and Calendar Accounts

The iPad works with iCloud, Microsoft Exchange, Gmail, Yahoo!, AOL, Hotmail and other popular email services. Here's how you set them up.

Setting Up Accounts

Apple's iCloud, Gmail and Microsoft Exchange not only provide free email, but also contacts and calendar information, plus you can sync to the iPad automatically and wirelessly. With iCloud, you can also sync your bookmarks on the iPad with Safari on your home PC or any other device running iOS 7.

For most of the popular email services, such as Gmail, the iPad will automatically enter most of the settings needed for you to access your account. That said, it is still a little complicated if you are unsure of what to do to set up an account on the iPad, so follow these steps for each of the key providers.

Setting Up an iCloud Email Account

Step 1 Tap the Setting icon located on the home screen of your iPad, and scroll down the left side panel and select Mail, Contacts, Calendars option. From here tap the Add Account option.

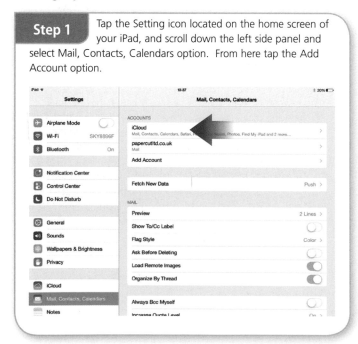

Step 2 From this screen tap on the iCloud link and enter your Apple ID and Password, these are the details you entered when you first set up your iPad. Tap Next to automatically verify your details.

Step 3 You now see a pop-up message, confirm you wish to give iCloud access to your location and use Find My iPhone, OK both and you will be taken to this screen, where you can select which apps use iCloud. Slide the Mail link to the On position.

Step 4 Having activated Mail with iCloud, now enter a username for your new @iCloud.com email address. The name you pick is up to you, but always choose something memorable. Once you have entered your details press Next and then confirm your details by pressing Done.

Setting Up a Gmail, Yahoo, AOL or Microsoft Outlook.com Email Account

NOTE: To access accounts from these email providers you must have already set up an active account with them. To do this you will need to visit their respective websites and follow the onscreen instructions.

Step 1 Tap the Setting icon located on the home screen of your iPad, and scroll down the right side and select Mail, Contacts, Calendars from the left hand panel of the Settings menu. From here tap the Add Account option.

Step 2 From this screen tap on either the Gmail, Yahoo, AOL or Microsoft Outlook.com link (The process is the same for them all).

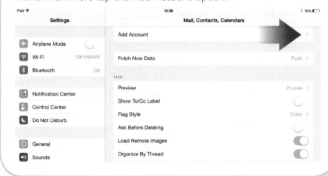

Step 3 On this screen you will need to enter your name, this name will be displayed to recipients of your emails. Next input your existing email address from one of the above providers and next your password for this account.

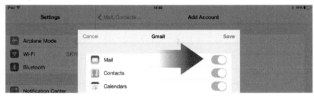

Finally enter a description of the account, this is useful if you intend to access numerous email accounts from your iPad. Click the Next link to continue.

Step 4 From this screen, you can select which features of your email account you also wish to sync with your iPad.

When you have made your selections, and are happy to continue, all you have to do to complete the process is tap the Save link and you are ready to go.

Setting Up Another, or a Microsoft Exchange, Email Account

Step 1 To start the process of collecting email on your iPad if your account is hosted with another provider than those listed on this screen or is hosted via Microsoft Exchange, you will need to tap either the Other or the Microsoft Exchange link respectively.

Step 2 You will have to visit the support website of your email provider and seek out their help in setting up either a POP or IMAP email account on your iPad As these details are all different for each provider, we can, alas, only send you in their direction for help.

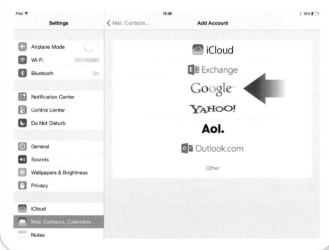

Getting More from Your iPad

Creating a Custom Signature for Your Emails

There is no reason why you have to stick with the standard signature that your iPad automatically adds to any emails. With a bit of work, you can create a unique HTML signature for your emails.

Alter a Basic Signature

Step 1   To change your signature, open the main Settings and scroll down to the Mail, Contacts, Calendars option.

Step 2   Scroll down and tap Signature to open the signature edit screen.

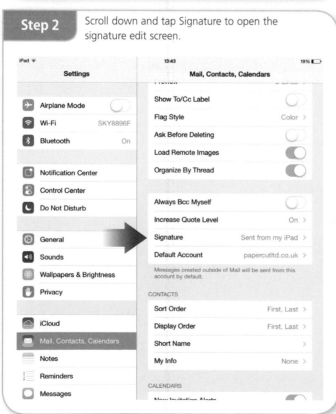

Step 3   In the edit box, type in whatever you want your signature to say and tap Done to finish.

Step 4   Your emails sent from your iPad will now end with your signature text.

Delete Multiple Emails at Once on Your iPad

If you have email delivered to your iPad, it can be annoying deleting several emails individually.
Here we take a look at how to delete multiple emails at once.

Step 1 When you check your email you may find you have several messages that you've already read on your computer, or that you just want to delete. Rather than go through and delete each one individually, you can select several and delete them at all once. Open your email and click the Edit button at the top.

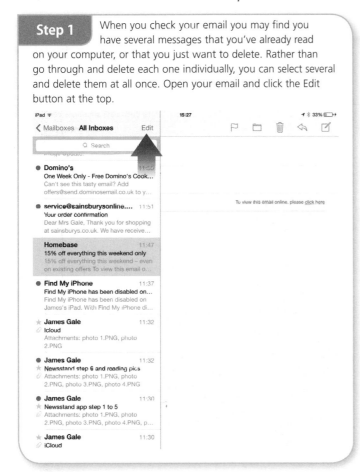

Step 2 Tap next to each email you want to delete and a red check-mark will appear, On the iPad these messages Will be listed as pages stacked to the right. After you've scrolled through and selected all the emails you want to get rid of, tap the Delete button at the bottom of the screen.

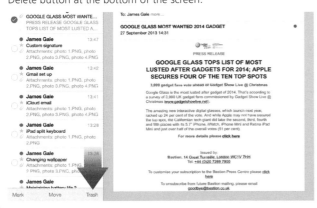

Step 3 If you're using Gmail or another client that supports the creation of folders you can also archive them or delete them by moving to the trash.

Step 4 If you prefer to delete your email individually, one trick is to go into Settings and turn off Ask Before Deleting. That way you won't have to deal with confirming you want to delete the mail when you tap on the trashcan icon.

That's all there is to it! If you have a lot of email you want to delete from your iOS device, this method makes it a lot easier.

How to use the
Email App

The ability to stay in touch via email from anywhere in the world is one of the main reasons to own an iPad. Let's take a look at this essential feature.

The Email App's key features explained

We've highlighted the key features of this application to help you understand better how it works.

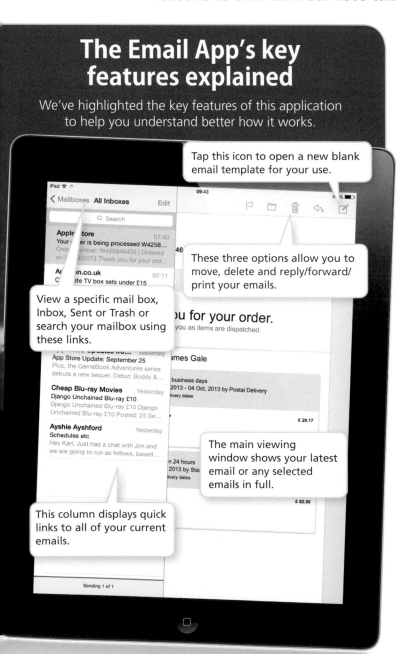

Tap this icon to open a new blank email template for your use.

These three options allow you to move, delete and reply/forward/print your emails.

View a specific mail box, Inbox, Sent or Trash or search your mailbox using these links.

The main viewing window shows your latest email or any selected emails in full.

This column displays quick links to all of your current emails.

Step 1 Tap the Mail icon to get started. This will bring up a list of email providers. Choose the relevant one. For example if you have a Yahoo! email account, select Yahoo! If your email host isn't displayed just tap Other.

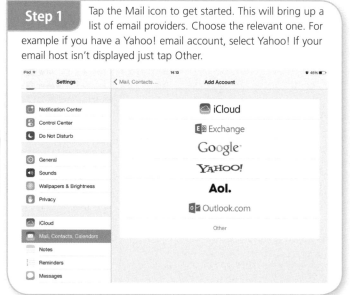

Step 2 Enter your name, email address and password and your account will be synced automatically.

Step 3 To sync more email accounts go into Settings, select Mail and choose Add Account. You'll then need to enter the name, address and password for the new account as before and it will be added to your list of inboxes when you open Mail.

Step 4 Tap the pen-and-paper icon to open a blank email. Enter an address manually by tapping the address field and typing. The field will automatically be filled by any matching contacts from your address book. If these are incorrect simply keep typing manually. To add a contact from your address book, tap the 'plus' symbol to go to your contact list. When you're done, just tap send.

Step 5 The Mail icon on the home screen will display the total number of unread emails you have. When you open Mail your inboxes will be displayed along with the number of unread emails in each. Select an inbox to read your emails.

Step 6 When you open an email you'll see several icons at the bottom of the screen. To move the email to a new folder tap the "Move" icon. To delete it tap "Trash".

Step 7 To search for a particular email, click on the text field at the top of the screen. Enter keywords here to search for them.

VIP Senders

It is widely agreed that iOS has long had one of the best email apps of any mobile operating system, combining ease of use with functionality. The iOS 7 update has further improved the email app by adding several cool new features, including VIP Senders.

Step 1 Open the Email app and find a message from someone you want to make a VIP Sender. Tap their name in the "from" field and you will be shown more details about them.

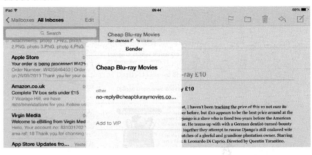

Step 2 As well as the familiar contact options, you will see a new button to Add to VIP. Tap this and a small star will appear next to their email address to show they have been added.

Step 3 Any new emails from people added as a VIP will now automatically be kept in a new VIP mailbox. You can remove VIP status by clicking their name in the "from" field and selecting Remove VIP.

Sending an Email

Now you are set up and ready to go with your email contact details, you will want to get started with the process of communicating with your contacts through the iPad's high quality email client - and this guide will show you how.

Step 1 Tap the Email Icon on your home screen to open the application.

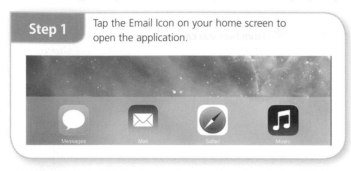

Step 2 Next tap the icon on the top right of the screen to open a new mail template.

Step 3 Enter the email address of the contact you wish to send the mail to in the "To:" bar at the top of the screen.

Step 4 Enter your subject line and the contents of your email via the keyboard and press the "Send" button.

Step 5 The progress bar at the bottom of the screen displays the percentage of the mail sent.

NOTE: If you are sending a very long email or an attachment, this will take noticeably longer than a short text-only email.

From the main email screen hit the Sent button and you will see your email displayed here.

Pull to Refresh

The small circular arrow icon, used to refresh your email inbox, has now disappeared in iOS 7. It has been replaced by Pull to Refresh, a feature that has been available in other apps (such as the Twitter app) for a while now. To refresh, simply drag your finger down the email list and release it when the stretchy icon snaps.

Replying To/Forwarding an Email

Communicating via email is a two-way process, so you'll want to know how to reply to messages you've received, and how to forward mail on to other recipients. As always, we're here to show you how.

Step 1 Open your Inbox and select the email you wish to reply to from the list of received mails, the newest being at the top. Now click the left point arrow icon on the top navigation bar to bring up the options tab.

Step 2 From here you can choose to Reply, Forward or Print your email. **NOTE: Forwarding an email allows you to resend the email to another person and follows the same process as detailed below to reply to an email.**

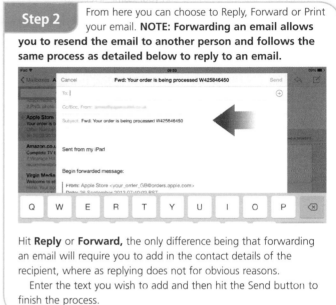

Hit **Reply** or **Forward,** the only difference being that forwarding an email will require you to add in the contact details of the recipient, where as replying does not for obvious reasons.

Enter the text you wish to add and then hit the Send button to finish the process.

Inserting Photos or Videos

Step 1 Open the email app and tap the New Message icon. Write the message you want to send and decide where you want to insert the image or video.

Step 3 Select the image or video you want to add from your camera roll (or other album) and then tap Use. The media is inserted into your message at the point where you touched.

Step 2 Touch and hold on the message wherever you want to insert the media. An action menu will appear giving you several options. Tap Insert Photo or Video.

How to use the
Safari App

Just tap the Safari icon to get started. If you've used Safari before, or any other browser for that matter, you're sure to feel at home right away.

Using the Safari App

Safari is Apple's very own web browser. If you've never used it before, here's a quick run through of the basics.

Step 1 To open Safari, tap the Safari icon on the home screen.

Step 2 To enter a web address manually, tap the text field to the top left of the screen to bring up the keyboard and then type in the address. Hit Go when you're done.

Step 3 To search Google, tap the smaller text field to the top right of the screen. Type in your keywords and hit Search. The results will then be displayed in Google with the most relevant results first.

Step 4 To return to the previous web page you were looking at, tap the left arrow at the top of the screen and to move to the next page tap the right arrow.

Step 5
To bookmark a page, tap the middle button at the top of the screen that shows an arrow coming out of a square. Tap **Add Bookmark**.

Step 6
You can add a short cut for any website to your home screen. To do this tap the arrow in a square button and choose **Add To Home Screen**. When you return to the home screen you'll see the web page you selected has appeared as an icon. Tap it to go straight the site.

To email a link to the currently selected site, tap the arrow-in-a-box button and select **Mail Link To This Page**. You will then be taken automatically to your email when you can choose a recipient (you'll need to have configured your email for this to work).

Step 7
If you wish to have more than one webpage open at any time, you can access the iPad's tabbed browsing option. To open another webpage without closing the one you are currently browsing tap the "+" icon at the top right of the screen. Now simply enter the web address you wish to visit as usual to open a new page. You can switch between these pages by tapping the corresponding "tab" displayed under the URL/Search bar. To close a tab tap the "X" icon at the far left of the bar.

Step 8
Pages can be oriented landscape or portrait by rotating the iPad.

Step 9 Tapping on any text field automatically brings up the keyboard. If you're filling in a text field and need to refer back to the webpage tap the keyboard icon to hide the keyboard.

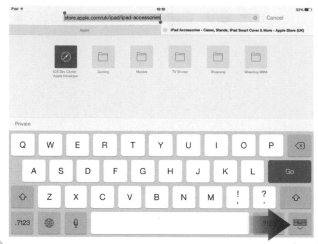

Step 10 You can set Safari up to automatically fill in online forms, saving you time when signing up with websites. Go to settings, select Safari and turn on Autofill.

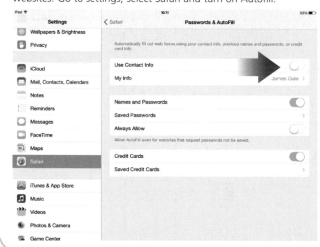

Step 11 Turn on the option Names & Passwords and Safari will remember all your website logins and passwords so you don't have to.

Find text on Safari Webpages

This unique version of the Safari browser for iPad adds some very impressive functionality. One of the most useful of these is the new ability to search within the text of webpages displayed in the browser.

Tap the URL bar of the Safari window and enter your search perimeters using the keyboard and when you are ready hit the Search key to begin.

Your search results will be displayed on this page, scroll to the bottom of the page, below the Google Search results to find the On This Page results. Tap this link and you will be taken to the first use of your keyword in the text on your current webpage.

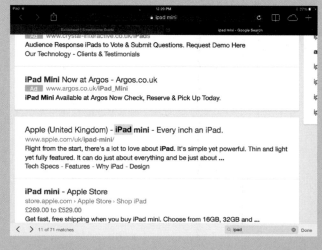

Using the arrows at the bottom left you can check each result in turn.

Using the Reading List

We will often find ourselves using the Safari web application when passing a few spare minutes, waiting for the bus or in a queue, and it is always these times that we manage to stumble upon something really interesting. Then of course the bus shows up and this nugget of Internet gold is lost forever. The Reading List feature was designed for exactly these moments, as it gives you the option to save the information for you to digest later. With this tutorial we will take you through the process, so you will never miss a thing on the world wide web.

Step 1
Open the Safari application and browse the Internet as normal.

Step 2
When you find something of interest that you want to give a little extra attention, click the the upward pointing arrow icon on the top bar to bring up the options tab.

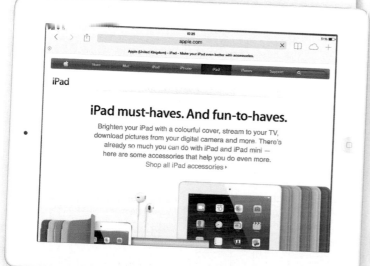

Step 3
From this menu tap "Add to Reading List" and the page will be saved for later viewing.

Step 4
To access your reading list tap the Bookmark icon the third from the right on the top navigation bar and your Reading List will be accessible as the top link.

Step 5
From this link you will see the listings of all sites you have added to the list, offering an icon and a few lines of content description to tweak your memory.

Step 6
Click one and you will taken directly to the page, read on...and enjoy!

Using the Internet on Your iPad

Using your iPad to browse the Internet literally opens up the entire world for you to explore and enjoy. With these tutorials we will show you how to go far beyond simple web browsing and use your Safari App to its full potential.

How to Connect to the Internet

The iPad will connect to the Internet automatically whenever you use the App Store, Mail, iTunes Store, Safari, YouTube or any other app that requires it. There are two ways in which this can be accomplished depending on the model you have; either via a Wi-Fi connection or via a 3G mobile network.

Joining a Wi-Fi network

To turn on the Wi-Fi on your iPad go to Settings > Wi-Fi and turn Wi-Fi on. Now you will need to join a Wi-Fi network. Once you have switched Wi-Fi on, the iPad will search for all networks in range. Depending on where you are, a variety of options may be available. If you are at home pick your home network and enter the security details to be allowed access. If you are at a public hotspot, it will either have no security and you can just connect, or you may need to find out the details from whoever is providing the Wi-Fi service.

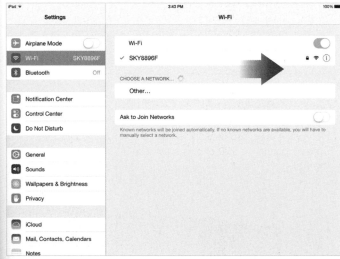

From now on whenever you are in range of this Wi-Fi service the iPad will automatically connect, without any prompting. If more than one is in range the iPad will join the last network it joined. There is a Wi-Fi indicator on the status bar at the top of the screen, depicting the signal strength, the more bars visible the stronger the signal.

Turn off duplicate SSIDs for Wi-Fi

There is a slight issue with the iPad recognising dual channel routers, this is one that uses 802.11a and 802.11n at the same time, when these two networks use the same name. So you will need to change the SSID of one of them so as not to confuse the iPad.

Joining a Mobile network

Before you can use your iPad on a 3G network you will need to sign up to a Mobile Service provider. Check your local retailers for price plans and availability. You can change or cancel this service at any time.

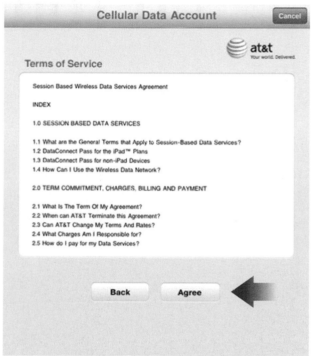

When the iPad connects to the Internet using the Mobile data network, you see the 3G, EDGE or GPRS icon in the status bar at the top of the screen.

If you travel outside your usual mobile network coverage you can still use the 3G functionality. To do this, turn Data Roaming on. But be aware roaming charges may apply. If you are not prepared to pay these charges make sure Data Roaming is turned off. You can monitor your Mobile network data usage by going to **Settings > Cellular Data > View Account**. Mobile data settings vary depending on the carrier. The iPad isn't locked to a specific provider, so you can sign up with whoever you wish.

Clear Cache, History and Cookies in Safari for iPad

Learn how to keep your browser activity private by clearing the cache, history and cookies stored in the Safari browser for iPad.

Step 1 Click on the main Settings icon on your iPad home screen.

Step 2 Choose Safari from the list of apps to see the settings specific to that app. Down near the bottom of the Safari settings you should see three options: Clear History, Clear Cache and Clear Cookies. Touching each of the buttons in turn will perform that action.

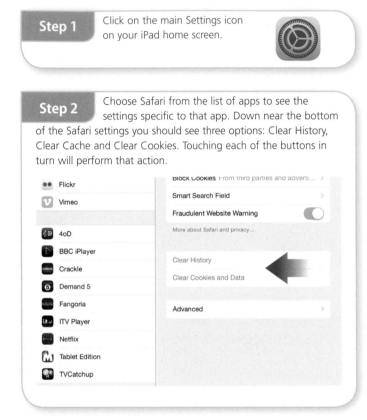

Step 3 Each time you press one of the buttons, a pop up will appear asking if you are sure you want to complete the action. Click Clear if you are sure you want to delete the information.

Step 4 With Cache, Cookies and History cleared, your browser will be reset to its default state. Perfect if you want to keep your browsing habits a secret.

Tabbed Browsing: An Introduction

As the iPad grows in speed, power and functionality, the gap between Apple's mobile hardware and the desktop computer narrows. In an attempt to bridge this gap even further Apple has introduced tabbed Safari web browsing to the iPad.

If you wish to have more than one web page open at any time, you can access the iPad's unique tabbed browsing option. To open another webpage without closing the one you are currently browsing tap the "+" icon at the top right of the screen. Now simply enter the web address you wish to visit as usual to open a new page. You can switch between these pages by tapping the corresponding "tab" displayed under the URL/Search bar. To close a tab tap the "X" icon at the far left of the bar.

Enable and Add to the Bookmarks Bar in Safari

This brief tutorial will show you how to display the Bookmarks Bar in Safari for the iPad and how to add bookmarks to it.

Step 1 Start out by selecting Settings from your home screen.

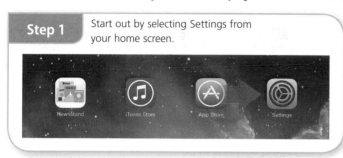

Step 2 Select Safari from the Settings column, and then slide the "Always Show Bookmarks Bar" switch to ON.

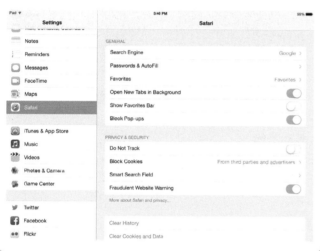

Step 3 Now launch Safari and visit a web site you want to have added to your Bookmarks Bar. Tap the + (plus sign) to add a bookmark and then tap in the space that says Bookmarks.

Step 4 Tap Bookmarks Bar.

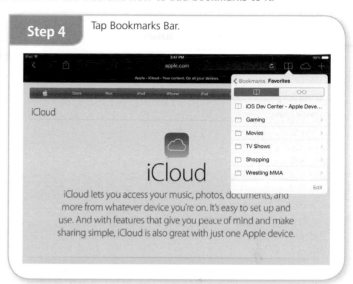

Step 5 You'll be taken back to the previous 'screen' and can now save the bookmark.

Step 6 It will now show up in the Bookmarks Bar for super-quick access.

f Using Facebook on Your iPad

Use this guide to get started with the official Facebook application, including setting up your account, searching for friends, uploading images and bringing your entire social network a little closer together.

Step 1 Signing up and signing in explained. With installation of the FaceBook app complete, you are given two options, Log in or Sign up. If you already have a Facebook account just enter your details as requested and press the "Go" button.

Step 2 Signing up to Facebook is simple, and you can do so via the iPad. Click Sign up to open a new window in Safari, and input the required details, confirming them via email and you are ready to go, now it's time to start finding some Friends.

Step 3 Click the Add Friends button at the bottom of the Home page, you have the option to either view suggestions, search, requests and contacts. Suggestions are people that you may know, search enables you to manually find your contacts.

Step 4 The remaining options, requests and contacts. The former being the link to any friend requests that you have received from people that know you and the latter will enable you to search the contacts lists from the listed options to see if any of these have a Facebook account.

Step 5
Having found the profile of the person you are searching for you can apply to add them to your friends lists and by return you will be added to theirs. To do this you will need to tap the "Add as Friend" button beside their contact name.

Step 6
Having sent your "friend request" to the specific individual you will only become linked to their friends list and you to theirs when they have accepted your request. You will be informed of this with a Notification which will appear at the top of the screen.

Step 7
There are two ways of socially interacting via Facebook. You can post your comments, images and links to your wall, to do this click your Profile link from the home page and select Update Status. Your post will now appear on your main profile page to be viewed by your friends.

Step 8
You can contact a friend directly by sending them a message, by clicking the Message link on the home page and tapping the new message icon in the upper left corner. Simply enter your message using the keyboard and tap Send.

Step 9
Staying in contact with your friends and family is the principal reason to use Facebook, yet there is a lot more for you to explore. Clicking the three lines icon in the top left corner will bring up all of your options, from your News Feed to Games.

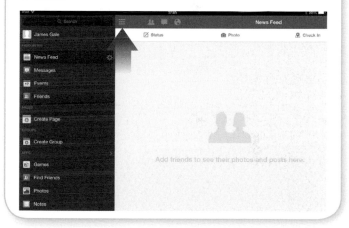

Step 10
You can add Photos to your Facebook page by tapping the Photos link from this menu and tap Create Album. Now tap the + icon in the top right corner and select the photos you wish to upload and then tap the Use link.

Using Facebook on Your iPad

When the iOS 5 update introduced much deeper Twitter integration to the iPad, there were many people who asked why Facebook hadn't been given the same treatment. Now iOS has answered those people by adding an even greater level of integration for the world's most popular social network.

Setting up Facebook Integration

Step 1 Facebook is now accessed via the Settings app. Scroll down to the bottom of the main apps list and tap the Facebook link. You will see that you have the option to install the official Facebook app. Do so now if you don't already have it installed.

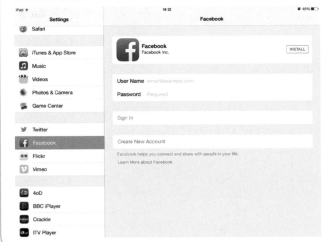

Step 2 To take full advantage of the new Facebook integration you need to sign in to your account using the sign in form in Settings. If you haven't already got a Facebook account, you can create a new one via the link below the sign in form.

Step 3 When you sign in, a pop-up window will open advising you which apps integrate with Facebook. Assuming you are happy with the information shown, tap Sign in. If you didn't install the Facebook app earlier, you will be prompted to do so now.

Step 4 Close Settings and tap the Facebook app icon. You will need to sign in to the app (even if you signed in through Settings) and then allow or refuse push notifications. If you have used the Facebook app before, it will look very familiar.

How to Use Facebook Integration

Sharing Images

You can quickly share images to your Facebook profile either through the Camera Roll or the iPhoto app. Simply open the image you want to post, tap the Share button and select the Facebook Icon. You can then add a title and description, as well as allowing the post to show your current location. Tapping the Friends icon allows you to choose the audience for your post.

Join Facebook to Contacts

You can now connect the people in your Contacts app with your friends in Facebook. As soon as you sign in, the contacts app will be populated with anyone you are friends with on Facebook. You can tell the difference between normal and Facebook contacts by the small f in the corner of the contact picture. You can easily turn off the feature in the Facebook settings.

Sharing Links

On the page you wish to share tap the Share button at the top of the browser window. Select the Facebook option and a pop-up window will open. As with images, a thumbnail is shown, and you have the option to add a title and description to the URL you are sharing. Also as with sharing images, you can add your location and choose your audience before you post.

Calendar Integration

Facebook for iOS 7 can now automatically add information to your Calendar app if you wish. Open Settings and tap the Facebook button to view the Facebook settings. Beneath the account login information you will see options to allow access to Contacts and Calendar. When you activate the calendar option, any information such as your friends' birthdays and events will automatically be added to your iOS calendar.

Post from Notifications

iOS 7 introduces the option to quickly start a new Facebook post via the Notifications panel. Drag your finger down from the top of the screen to open the Notifications panel and you will see two new buttons: Tap to tweet for Twitter and Tap to Post for Facebook. The Tap to Post button will open a new window which will allow you to post to your timeline.

Post Using Siri

If you have a new iPad (a 3rd generation iPad) you have access to Siri, Apple's personal assistant app. Siri is now fully integrated with Facebook, so you can post a status update using just your voice. To get Siri to post for you, activate Siri and say something like "Post to Facebook, holiday starts tomorrow" or "Write on my wall, it's time to party!" Confirm the post and it will appear on Facebook.

How to use the Twitter App

Whether it's celebrity gossip, the latest breaking news or just a friendly chat, it sometimes seems that the whole world is on Twitter.

The Twitter App's Key Features Explained

We've highlighted the key features of this application to help you understand better how it works.

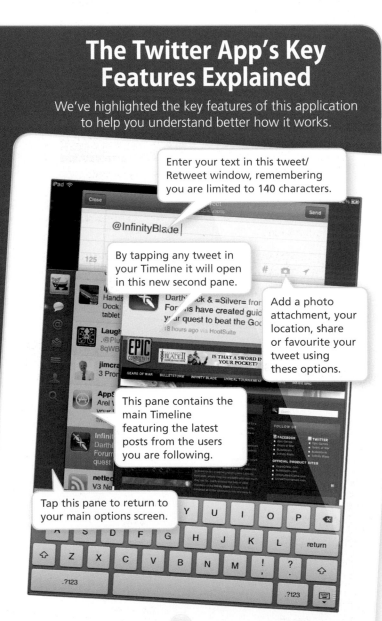

Enter your text in this tweet/Retweet window, remembering you are limited to 140 characters.

By tapping any tweet in your Timeline it will open in this new second pane.

Add a photo attachment, your location, share or favourite your tweet using these options.

This pane contains the main Timeline featuring the latest posts from the users you are following.

Tap this pane to return to your main options screen.

Using Twitter on iOS

Step 1 Select the content you wish to share, tap the right pointing arrow icon at the top of the screen and select the "tweet" option.

Step 2 You will now see the file you wish to share displayed as shown here. You can add any required text and your location and when you are ready to send the tweet tap the "Send" link.

Step 3 Your tweet will now be shared with your followers, you can log into the Twitter app to confirm this.

Your Guide to Using the Twitter App

This guide to the official Twitter app covers installation, searching for and following other users, and tweeting your latest thoughts or opinions, although it may take more than 140 characters to explain!

Getting Started

Step 1 Upon opening this app for the first time you will be greeted with a lot of information, but don't panic! On the left you will notice the categories that your fellow Twitter users fall under.

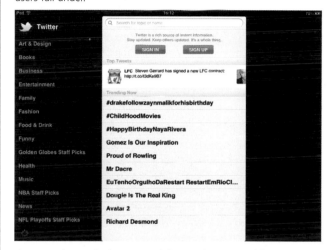

The central area displays a search bar at the top, enabling you to search for specific content in others' posts.

Below this are the "Sign In" and "Sign Up" buttons and finally some links to the most popular "Trending" topics of the moment.

Signing Up/In for Twitter

Step 2 If you are a new user, you can sign up for an account by tapping the relevant button and entering the requested information, and thus confirming your details through the linked email address.

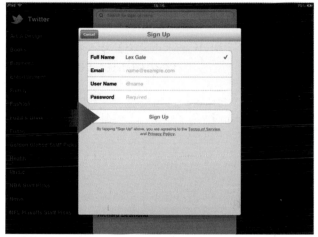

Having completed the sign up you can now search your iPad's contacts list to directly link to their Twitter accounts or simply browse categories of personal interest, if you see any areas of interest simply click the "follow" button on the right side of the link to follow this user.

Following Users

Step 3

If you wish to follow a specific user, enter their name into the search bar to locate them, then if you require more information before following, a quick tap on their info bar will bring up their full profile and their timeline.

Again if you are interested in following this user simply tap the follow button.

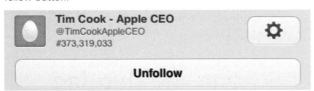

If you have an existing account, simply sign in and you will be taken to your main page, with your current timeline displayed and various options on the menu hub below.

The Timeline

Step 4

Having signed into your account, you will notice that you have six options available, the default display for the main screen being your Timeline. This shows the tweets of the users you are following and any tweets you have made yourself, flowing downward based upon the time the comment was posted.

Scroll down this list by gesturing downward on the pane. To focus on a single tweet simply tap the screen to open the relevant link.

Further Options

Step 5

Your remaining options are:

Mentions – a listing of any posts that contain your user name in them.

Messages – any private messages that have been sent to you from other users.

Lists – group together similar theme users you are following.

Profile – edit your profile or upload a new avatar.

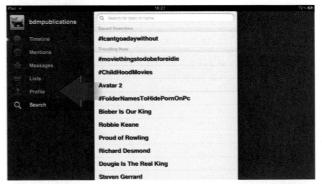

Search – search for a user, theme or item to reveal any tweets on that subject, all searches can be saved and accessed from this link.

Settings Explained

Step 6 The Settings option enables you to personalise your Twitter experience when you are offline, or to close your account. To do the latter you have to return to the iPad's main Settings menu and select Twitter, then User Name, and then hit the "Delete Account" button.

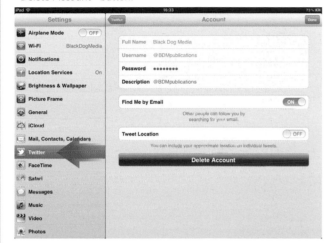

Notifications configures your Push messages – the pop-ups that appear much like a text message – that alert you of personal messages, mentions and replies to your previous tweets.

Advanced settings control image and video quality and delivery and we advise you to leave these at default.

Tweeting Explained

Step 7 To "tweet" tap the New Message icon – the same icon used when emailing or instant messaging – to reveal the "New tweet" pane at the top of the screen and the keyboard at the bottom. Enter your thoughts and press "Send" to add the comment to your timeline. The four icons on the right side of this pane are used as follows. The @ icon enables you to direct a comment at a specific user you are following. The # symbol directs your tweet at a specific topic thread. The camera icon allows you to attach an image to your tweet and the arrow symbol adds a geotag to your tweet, which shows your location when the comment was made.

Retweeting and Quoting

Step 8 If you retweet or quote a post from another user, it will be added to your timeline at the point you retweeted or quoted, and not when the post was originally made. To do this, open the user pane and tap the two arrows icon located by the user name. When quoting, the user comment will be attributed to your personal account and sent out to all of your followers, while a retweeted comment will remain attributed to the original poster and remain in your Timeline only.

How to use the Notifications App

iOS 7's notification system makes keeping track of new notifications and acting on them very quick and simple.

The Notification App's Key Features Explained

We've highlighted the key features of this application to help you understand better how it works.

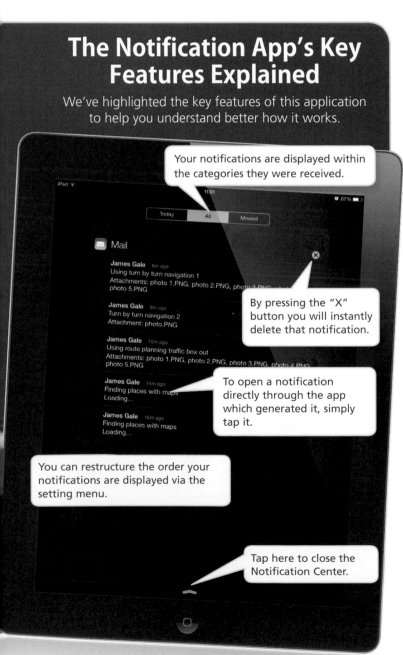

Your notifications are displayed within the categories they were received.

By pressing the "X" button you will instantly delete that notification.

To open a notification directly through the app which generated it, simply tap it.

You can restructure the order your notifications are displayed via the setting menu.

Tap here to close the Notification Center.

Step 1 You can access the new Notification Center at any time, no matter what app you're in, simply by swiping your finger down from the top of the screen.

When you swipe down, Notification Center will be pulled into view and you'll be able to see all your current notifications.

Step 2 To clear notifications that you don't want to deal with, all you have to do is tap the cross next to the appropriate one and then tap Clear when prompted. This will remove the notification enabling you to keep Notification Center tidy and uncluttered.

Confirming Content for Notifications

Now you know where and how to access Notification Center and its various functions, but there are also several options you can use to further tailor it to your liking. Using these guides will help you get the most from this application.

Step 1 To access the Notification options from the home screen tap Settings.

Step 2 Scroll down the list of functions and apps until you see Notification Center then tap it. This is where you can configure Notification Center to work the way you want it to.

Step 3 You can have notifications listed chronologically in the order they appeared or you can choose to group them by app so all new notifications from a specific app appear together.

Step 4 Select Time to have notifications displayed chronologically. This way you'll see all your notifications displayed in the order in which they were received with the most recent at the top.

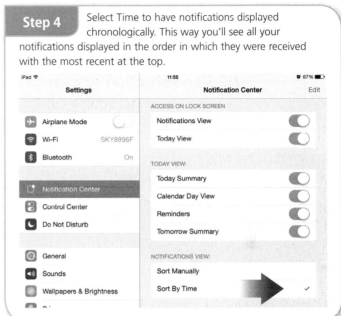

Step 5 If you would prefer to group your notifications by the app from which they were generated, tap the Edit button.

Step 6 You'll see that a symbol showing three horizontal lines has appeared next to each app name. Holding your finger on this symbol and then sliding it up and down enables you to drag the app to the desired position in the list. For example if you choose to place it second in the list behind Mail then all Mail notifications will appear first in Notification Center followed by all notifications from the app you selected.

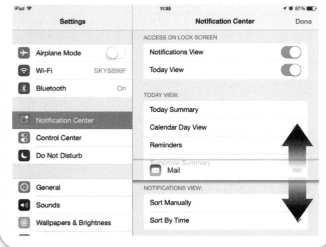

Step 7 When you're happy with the order in which your apps appear tap the Done button.

Step 8 To adjust the notification settings for any individual app, just tap on the app title. You'll then be able to choose how you want notifications from that app to be handled.

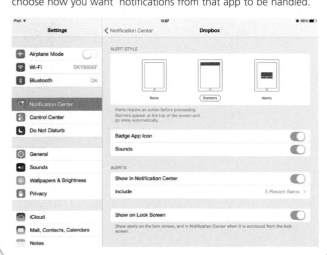

Step 9 If you don't want to receive alerts from a particular app, tap on its name then turn its notifications off.

Step 10 If at any time you want to turn on notifications for an app you previously turned off, just click on the app name in settings and switch it back on. Notifications from that app will then appear in Notification Center as before.
Tap the back arrow when you're happy with your choices to return to the main screen.

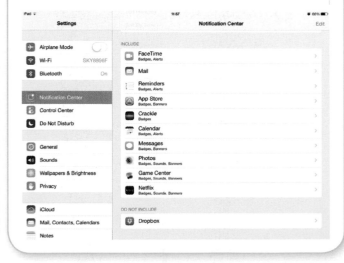

Accessing Notifications
from the Lock Screen or when in use

If you receive notifications when your iPad is locked they will appear on the lock screen. This way you don't have to go into Notification Center to check for new notifications every time you look at your iPad.

Step 1 You can access notifications straight from the lock screen by tapping the notification alerts to reveal a slider. While still holding the the notification slide from left to right in exactly the same way you use the 'slide to unlock' button to unlock your iPad normally. Doing this takes you directly to the app for which the notification appeared.

Step 2 If there were multiple notifications on the lock screen you can review them by entering Notification Center as normal by swiping down from the top of the screen.

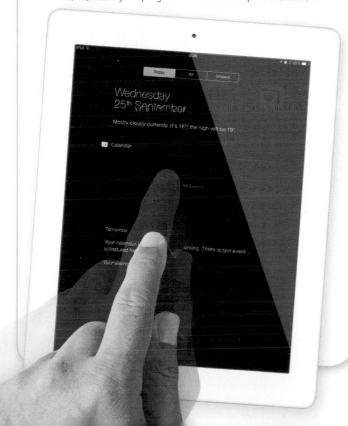

Step 3 If a notification is generated by any app while your iPad is in use it will appear as an alert at the top of the screen. Unlike the old notification system it won't pause or affect what you're doing in any way. To act on it immediately just tap it to be taken straight to the relevant app.

Step 4 If you don't want to act on it immediately or you're busy, don't worry. Just ignore it and after a few seconds it will disappear.

Step 5 When you are ready to deal with your message, tap the home button and swipe down from the top of the screen to open the Notification Center and you will find it waiting for you.

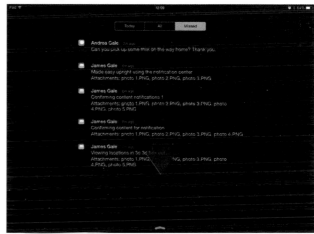

7 The A-Z of iPad
Mini Guides

The iPad considered by many to be the best tablet in the world, and rightly so. It can take a while to fully get to grips with such a powerful tablet and operating system, and without a little help many of the little tricks and hidden features can remain a mystery. This huge collection of iPad and iOS tips is your shortcut to making the iPad work the way you want and need it to, without having to do any of the hard work.

A

Album Artist

If you have a lot of albums which feature tracks by more than one artist, you have probably been annoyed at the way the Music app groups them by Artist rather than Album. With iOS, this little frustration can be a thing of the past. Open Settings > Music, toggle Group By Album Artist on and albums with multiple artists will now be grouped into one listing in the Music app.

Alert Badges

Many apps, such as Messages, Mail, and the App Store, can display an alert badge on their Home screen icon with either a number to indicate incoming items or an exclamation mark to indicate a problem. If these apps are contained in a folder, the badge appears on the folder. You can turn off alert badges in the Notifications menu in Settings.

Autofocus with a Tap

The camera app, at first glance, seems very simple with few controls. This is because Apple has designed it to be point and click, and to make taking good snaps as easy as possible. Autofocus is one tool that the app uses to help you. If you want to turn Autofocus off, for whatever reason, you can do so by tapping and holding anywhere on the camera screen. You will see "AF/AE Lock" on screen. Repeat to turn it back on.

B

Backup Automatically

You can use iCloud or iTunes to automatically back up your iPad. If you choose to automatically back up using iCloud, you can't also use iTunes to automatically back up to your computer, but you can use iTunes to manually back up to your computer. iCloud automatically backs up to iPad daily over Wi-Fi, when it's connected to a power source and is locked (when charging for example). To enable iCloud Backup, open Settings > iCloud > Storage & Backup.

Big Hands, Small Keys

If you find typing on the iPad keyboard a bit cramped, try tilting the iPad into landscape view. The keyboard stretches out to fill the wider angle and the keys should become a little easier to hit accurately.

C

Cleaning Your iPad

Before cleaning your iPad, disconnect all cables and switch off by pressing and holding the On/Off button, then sliding the on-screen slider. To clean the outer shell use a soft, slightly moist, lint-free cloth. Avoid getting moisture in the ports and openings.

The front cover of iPad is made of glass and has an oleophobic coating. To clean these surfaces, simply wipe with a soft, dry, lint-free cloth.

Customise the Home Screen

Although the grid layout of the iPad home screen is pretty much the only option, there is no reason not to get things set up in a way that makes sense for you. Tap and hold anywhere on the home screen until the icons start to jiggle. You can then move them around, including onto the dock, and group them into folders by dropping one icon onto another

D

Default Mail Account

Various iOS apps use your default email address to send out communications. YouTube uses it to share links, and Photos uses it to post images. Your default address is usually whichever one you set up first, but, if you want to change it, open Settings >Mail, Contacts and Calendars, Scroll down to Default Account and choose an alternative.

Delete by Swiping

The iOS mail app (along with many other apps that use a list format) allows you to quickly delete an item by swiping across it from left to right. When you do this, a delete button appears to confirm the action.

Don't Notify Me

If you are getting fed up with all the apps, games and services sending notifications, you can turn them off individually in the Settings. Tap Settings > Notifications and you will see a list of all the apps that use notifications. Tap the slider next to each app you want to stop bugging you with updates.

Double-Tap Space

Another handy keyboard shortcut is the double-tap spacebar to insert a full stop (followed by a space). This isn't going to change your life, but once you get used to doing it, you will wonder why you ever messed around opening the punctuation keys on the keyboard.

E Edit Conversations

Email conversations can get incredibly long and finding something in a long conversation can be a pain. If you want to keep just part of a conversation, you can delete the parts you don't want. You can also delete entire conversations from the Messages list. Open the conversation and tap Edit, select the parts to delete, then tap Delete.

F Finger Slide

As you type, each letter appears above your thumb or finger. If you touch the wrong key, you can slide your finger to the correct key. The letter isn't actually entered until you release your finger from the key.

G Get Purchase History

Over the life of your iPad, you will

almost certainly download and then delete dozens of apps, either because you don't want them any more, or to save space. Thanks to iCloud, if you want to get any of those apps back onto your phone, the app store lets you see not only apps that are on your device, but also apps that no longer are. Open the App Store, tap Updates and then Purchased. Tap the Not on This iPad tab and you can view all previously purchased apps. Tap the iCloud icon to download any app in the list.

I iCloud Backup

As you are new to the iPad, remember that an Apple ID comes with 5GB of free storage in your iCloud account. Before you can take advantage of this service, you will need to set it up. Head to Settings > iCloud > Storage & Backup and make sure "iCloud Backup" is toggled on. Any time you're plugged in, locked and on a Wi-Fi connection, the device will back up your precious Camera Roll, accounts, documents and settings without having to think about it.

iCloud Refund

If you've paid for additional storage but you're coming nowhere close to needing it all, reduce it. In some territories, Apple will even give you a partial refund. Tap Settings > iCloud > Account and then view the details of your storage plan. You should then see Downgrade Options.

Increase Text Size

If you are struggling to read the text of Emails, Notes or Messages, there are several different solutions. These include altering individual app settings and using pinch to zoom. If you want a simple all-in-one solution, the Large Text option is worth a try. Open Settings > General > Accessibility. Tap the Large Text option and choose the size you want. This will be applied to almost all text on the phone.

J Just a Name?

If you've copied your iPad data to a new tablet every time you've updated,

your device name may be completely wrong for the model you're currently using. Change this so that it's correctly identified in the iTunes sidebar through Settings > General > About > Name.

K Keyboard Shortcut Customisation

Custom keyboard shortcuts are great for email addresses, long names or place names that you type regularly. For example, if your email is MrWarburton@verylongemailaddress.com, you could enter "me@" as a shortcut. Now, whenever you want to enter your email address, type Me@ and the iPhone will automatically suggest your email address. Go to Settings > General > Keyboards to set up your shortcuts.

L Local Weather

By default, the weather app will show the weather only in the main towns and cities of your country. Even if you have Location Services turned on, this won't show your local weather unless you tell it to. Open the Weather app and tap the tiny info icon at the bottom of the screen. This lets you turn on Local Weather and also set specific locations for weather reports.

Lock the Caps Lock

Caps Lock switching back to lower case after the first letter has been typed is usually a good thing. However, it can be a little bit awkward if you want to type a whole word in capitals. A surprising number of iPad uses don't realise that you can lock caps by double-tapping the button. When you do this it will turn blue and everything you write will be in capitals until you tap the button again.

M Manage Web Data

If you want to know how much storage space websites are taking up on your device, open Settings > Safari > Advanced and tap Website Data. Each site that stores data will be shown here. You can delete the worst websites, displayed at top, or scroll to the bottom and tap Remove All Website Data.

Manage Your iBooks

If your iBooks collection is getting out of control and the shelves are towering above the top of the screen, some tidying needs to be done. Organise your books into more logical collections on the basis of subject, author, read status or whatever suits you best. Tap Books and then New to define a new collection. Now, to file your books, return to your shelves and tap Edit. Select the books you want to move to your new collection and tap Move. Select the collection from the screen that pops up to complete the move.

N Night Reading Mode
The newest version of iBooks includes a useful "Night Reading" mode, which switches the text from black on white to white on black. The contrast makes it easier to read the text in low light. By using the Accessibility settings, you can enable a similar option for any text, from emails to web pages. Open Settings > General > Accessibility > Triple Click Home and select Toggle White on Black. Now, when you are reading any dark text on a white background, triple click on Home and the screen will switch to white on black.

O OTA Updates
Previously, iOS devices had to be plugged into a computer with iTunes to have the system software updated. With the launch of iOS 5 that changed and updates can now be downloaded and installed without you ever having to plug into a computer. To check for and download updates, open Settings and tap Software Update. Your iPad will check for any available software updates and if found they can be downloaded at the touch of a button.

P Power Button Problems
If the Sleep/Wake button does not seem to be working as it should (waking the tablet when pressed, etc.), you should first try resetting the iPad. Press and hold the Sleep/Wake button for a few seconds until a red slider appears, and then slide the slider. Now press and hold the Sleep/Wake button until the Apple logo appears.

Press and Hold Keyboard
Even if you have the English keyboard selected, pressing and holding certain keys will pop up additional options for that letter (German punctuation such as the umlaut for example). There are also several options for many of the punctuation keys including a quick way to type "..."

Q Quick Email Delete
Instead of opening each bit of junk mail, tapping Delete and Delete again, remember that you can get rid of several at once. Go into the mailbox you want to clean up, tap Edit and then select all of the emails you want to get rid of. When they are all selected, tap Delete to remove them all in one go.

R Reset , Reset, Reset
Lots of the things you can customise on your iPad can easily be reset to their factory defaults if you should need to at any time. Open Settings > General > Reset and you will see that you can reset all settings, network settings, keyboard dictionary, home screen layout and location warnings. You can also use this menu to erase all content on the iPad. Just be aware that once the settings have been reset, they are gone for good and you will have to start all over again.

S Searching For...
You can search within many of the apps on iPad, including Contacts, Mail, Calendar, Music, Messages, Notes, and Reminders. You can search an individual app, or all apps at once. Search results appear as you type. Tap an item in the list to open it. Tap Search to dismiss the keyboard and see more results. Icons next to the search results show which app the results are from. Scroll right to the bottom of the results and you will see the option to search the web or search Wikipedia.

Speak Any Text
Your iPad features the option to read aloud any text that you select. By default, this option is turned off, so head into Settings > General > Accessibility and turn on Speak Selection. Now give it a try. Open any app that has text, Mail for example, highlight some text and you will see an option to Speak. Tap this and the text is read out to you. You can alter the speed that the text is read out in the Accessibility Settings.

Sync to YouTube
If you have a YouTube account containing all your favourites and playlists, you can sync it with your phone so that all of the content is shown when you open the app. To sync to your account, open the YouTube app and tap More and then tap Sign In. Enter your YouTube account details and your favourites, playlists and uploaded videos will be instantly accessible.

T Take a screenshot
There are any number of reasons why you might want to save a image of the information on your iPhone screen, showing off about our incredible Bejewelled scores being one of our favourites! To take a screenshot of anything on your iPad, press and hold the Sleep/Wake button, then press the Home button. You will hear a camera shutter sound and the screen will flash white.

Tap for Definitions
With a couple of taps of your finger, you can check the dictionary definition of any word you type, see on a web page or receive in an email or message. Tap the word you want to check and then tap Define from the contextual menu that pops up. The iOS 5 built in dictionary will open, showing you the definition of the word. When you are finished reading, tap Done to go back to what you were doing.

Travel Direction
When you are looking at your location in Maps, it is shown as a blue dot. If you are trying to navigate to a particular location you can check which direction you are travelling in by tapping the compass icon at the bottom of the screen. This allows you to easily see the direction you are currently facing.

Turn off Auto-Brightness
Using the Ambient Light Sensor, your iPad intelligently detects how much light is reaching it and alters the brightness of the screen accordingly. This is generally a good system and works well for many users. If, however, you are looking at ways to preserve the battery, turning off Auto-Brightness and selecting a fixed mid-level instead can help. Look in Settings > Brightness.

U USB Charging
The iPad battery may drain instead of charge if it is connected to a computer

that's turned off or is in sleep or standby mode. It is also worth remembering that if you charge the battery while syncing or using iPad, it will usually take longer to charge.

Use the Grid

The iPad Camera app now includes a Grid to help you compose your photos better. Lining up the horizontal or vertical lines with elements seen on the screen will help to avoid wonky pictures. You can also follow the rule of thirds for all-round better photographs. Open the Settings app and tap Photos & Camera and turn Grid on and off from here.

V Video Converting

You can add videos other than those purchased from the iTunes Store to your iPad, such as videos you create in iMovie on a Mac, or videos you download from the Internet and then add to iTunes. Sometimes you will see a message that says the video can't play on iPad, in which case you will need to convert it. Select the video in your iTunes library and choose Advanced > Create iPod or iPhone Version. Wait for the process to finish and add the converted video to iPad. Simple!

Voice Dialling When Locked

Unless you tell it not to, your iPhone will allow Voice Dialling even when it is locked with a passcode. This means that should your phone fall into the wrong hands, it could be used to make calls (Voice Dialling lets you speak the numbers, not just names in your Contacts) and you could end up with a huge bill. Go to Settings > General > Passcode Lock and turn Voice Dial off. You will now need to unlock your phone before you can use voice dial.

Volume Up Shutter Control

With iOS 5 installed on your iPad, you can use the physical volume up button as the camera app shutter control. Whilst the on screen shutter button works fine in most situations, there might be occasions when being able to use a button on the edge of the tablet is easier or quicker.

W Web Clips

A handy way to give yourself easy access to your favourite websites is to create Web Clips. Web Clips are simply home screen shortcuts to a particular web page. Browse to the site you want to save in Safari

and then tap the Save As button (curved arrow in a box). Select Add to Home Screen and give your Web Clip a title. Tap Add and it will appear on the home screen as a clickable icon. Some sites have a custom icon for Web Clips, whilst others just use a thumbnail of the page.

What's in a Voice

When using the iPad's voice assistant Siri, you have the option to change the gender of the voice. By opening the Settings app and then open General. From here tap Siri and then tap Voice. You can now change the voice from Male to Female depending on your preference.

Who's On iMessage?

Your iPad and iOS 5 makes it easy for you to see who's on iMessage and who's using traditional SMS to connect. iMessage users will show a blue Send button, with the word "iMessage" displayed in an empty text field. Likewise, old-school SMS users will have a green Send button with the words "Text Message" in an empty text field.

Wi-Fi Security

If you are in the habit, as many people are, of leaving your Wi-Fi connection on at all times, it is possible that your iPad will connect to unsecured open networks when you are away from home. This can be a security issue, even though your iPad is just trying to be efficient and helpful. To make sure that you are always asked before the device connects to an unknown network, open Settings > Wi-Fi and turn on Ask to Join Networks.

Y Wi-Fi Sync

To enable wireless syncing, plug you iPad into your computer and open iTunes. Check the "Sync with this iDevice over Wi-Fi" option in iTunes. On the iPad, open Settings > General > iTunes Wi-Fi Sync and tap "Sync Now" and you can initiate a sync while you're not sat at your computer.

Your Store

You can replace the Music, Podcasts, Videos, and Search buttons at the bottom of the iTunes Store screen with ones you use more frequently. For example, if you download audio books often but don't watch many videos, you could replace Videos with Audio books. Tap More, tap Edit, then drag a button to the bottom of the screen, over the button you want to replace.

Z Zoom with Pinch

Pinch to Zoom is not just for viewing text and web pages you know. While framing a photo in the Camera app, simply use the familiar two-finger pinch to zoom into or out of your shot. For those who prefer the old style, the normal zoom slider will pop up once you initiate a pinch to zoom.

Zoom with Three Fingers

If you want to be able to increase the size of icons or text in certain apps, but don't want to increase the font size for everything on your iPad, Accessibility give you a simple but effective solution. Open Settings > General > Accessibility and turn on Zoom. This allows you to selectively zoom anything on your screen by simply double-tapping the screen with three fingers. You can then scroll around the screen in any direction, also using three fingers.

iPad User Guides & Tutorials

Over these pages we will take on a journey, starting as an iPad novice, and hopefully ending up as an iPad expert. With our collection of user-friendly and highly detailed guides and tutorials, covering every major element of your daily iPad use, no matter what problems you face we are going to be here to help you solve them.

CONTENTS...

How to use the Siri Application

Siri, the digital assistant available with iOS 7 on the iPad and iPad mini, can be a powerful and useful tool, but only if you take the time to understand how it works

Siri Lets Your Voice Do The Work...

Although voice recognition software has been around for a long time, you will probably have never encountered anything quite like Siri! Representing a huge leap forward in voice recognition technology, Siri is frankly amazing, an app that will literally answer your questions and complete tasks for you by voice command. To help you experience Siri for yourself on your iPad, follow these simple tutorials on its use.

Can I Use Siri?

Siri does much more than just help you. Whether it's making a call, scheduling reminders and meetings, searching the web or dictating text there is very little Siri can't do. You should note that Siri is only available on the new iPad, running iOS 7. Users of earlier models can use third party speech-to-text apps such as Dragon Diction which is available from the App Store for free. You will also need Internet access via Wi-Fi or 3g/4G, so before using this app we suggest you contact your service provider regarding potential charges.

Asking Siri a Question Explained

Tasks which seem simple can still often run into problems, but with help from Siri they can be made much simpler. The knowledge available via Siri is simply amazing. What follows is a short tutorial showing you how to access this wealth of information.

Step 1 To access Siri, press and hold the Home button. The app will automatically launch and you will be greeted with a question of your own from Siri, "What can I help you with?"

Step 2 That question is your cue to ask your question. Depending on the level of background noise you may need to hold your iPad close to your mouth so that Siri can hear you clearly..

Step 3 Siri will repeat your question back to you, and then attempt to answer it,

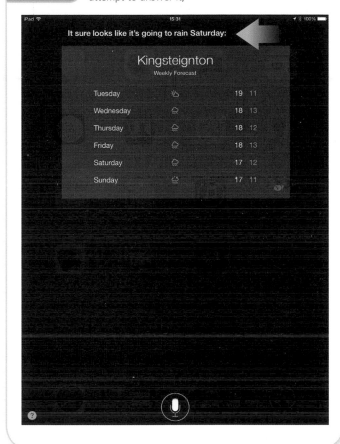

Step 4 Should it be required, Siri will open any applications it needs in order to answer your question. For example if you asked a question regarding the temperature it will open the Weather application.

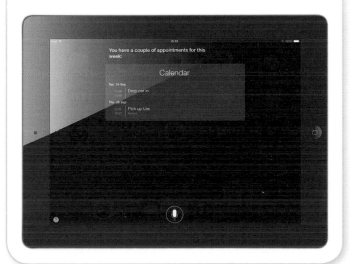

Step 5 On the rare occasions that Siri isn't able to answer a question, it will suggest making a web search. To instantly access this search simply click the on-screen icon

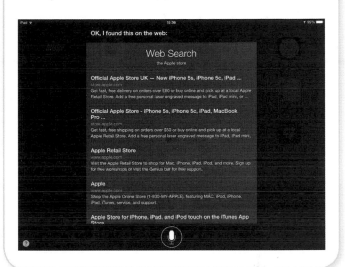

Step 6 You will be transferred to the Safari web browser which will already have your search results and hopefully your answer.

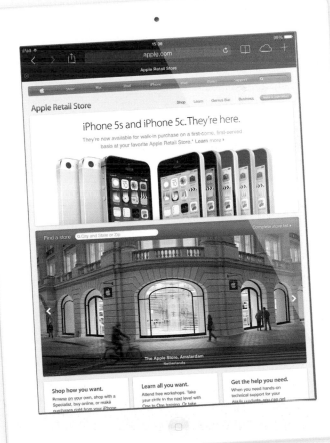

Teaching Siri

For Siri to work to its full potential you need to spend a little bit of time teaching it a few things.

Who's Who?

The first thing to do is teach it who's who in your life. You can say something like "Kari is my wife" to Siri and as long as that person is in your contacts, Siri will ask if you want to save that information. Kari will then be added as "Spouse" on your contact card. You can then use commands like "tell my wife I'll be home late". You may think this a bit pointless, but it is usually easier for Siri to understand "Wife" or "Brother" than a name.

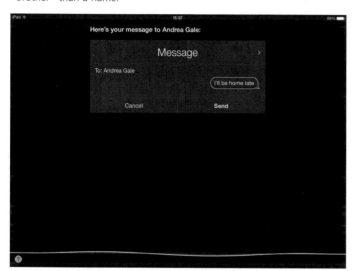

Contacts

To help Siri to help you, make sure that your Contacts app (including your own contact card) contains as much information as possible. Your contacts list doesn't just need to include mobile phone numbers. You can add numerous addresses, email details, Twitter names, Facebook pages, birthdays and much more. The more information you can include, the more useful Siri will be.

Important Addresses

Tell Siri your home and work address so it can be used to set reminders when you arrive at or leave. You can also tell it other important addresses such as your girlfriend's house, etc. You can then use commands like "Remind me to get milk when I leave work".

Voice Recognition

The more you use Siri, the better it will understand you. It does this by learning about your accent and other characteristics of your voice. Siri uses voice recognition algorithms to categorise your voice into one of the dialects or accents it understands.

Apps Siri Works With

Siri is able to interact with many of the built-in iOS apps, as well as an increasing number of third-party apps. Built-in apps that Siri works with include:

- Reminders
- FaceTime
- Notes
- Music
- Contacts
- Mail
- Weather
- Messages
- Stocks
- Calendar
- Web Search
- Alarms
- World Clock
- Timer
- Wolfram Alpha
- Wikipedia Search

12 Great ways to use Siri

Checking Appointments

Siri can tell you if you have any appointments on any particular date or even in a time frame. Say to Siri something like "What's my schedule for April?" and it will tell you how many appointments you have in that month and list them on screen. If you want to be more specific, say "What are my appointments today" or "What's my schedule for June 19th?"

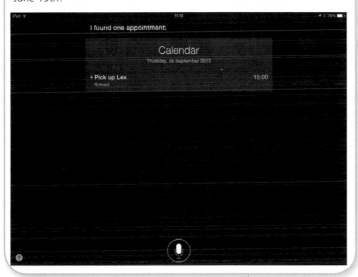

Turning Alarms On or Off

Siri is designed to make common tasks easier, but there are some things that you just might not think about using your personal assistant to do. Rather than fumbling about late at night to turn your morning alarm on or off, simply raise the phone to your ear, wait for the beeps and say "Turn on (or off) my alarm". Siri will confirm the action and you can get to sleep knowing that you won't be late for work.

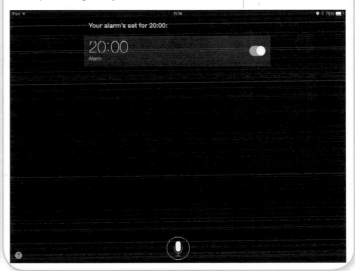

Creating a Secure Password

Say "Wolfram, password." Wolfram generates a difficult-to-crack random 8-character password. You can then scroll down for a list of alternatives. Scroll further down and you can even see how difficult the password is to crack for hackers using known decryption methods.

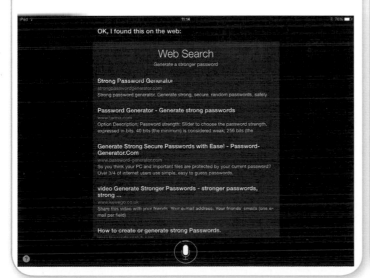

Adding Things Up

Siri is particularly good at maths questions, from general things like "What is six multiplied by nine?" to more real-world problems such as splitting a restaurant bill, "What is ninety six divided by five?" If that isn't impressive enough for you, try something harder like "What is the square root of 45,051?"

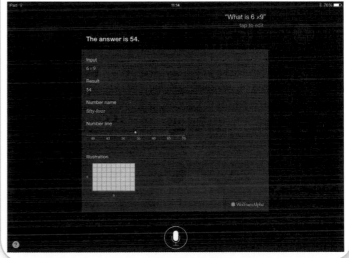

Looking Things Up

Siri works with normal web search, Wikipedia search and Wolfram Alpha (more for scientific questions). To look things up, speak to Siri as you would to anyone you were asking a question of. What is the average size of a polar bear? Which planet is the largest? Why does snow fall? Siri will use the source it thinks best able to answer the question. If you want to use a particular search engine, simply say the name before the question "Wolfram, how far is it to the Sun?".

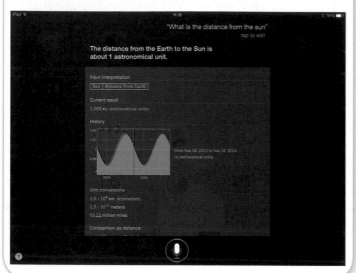

Playing Music

Siri will quite happily find and play your music at your command. You can tell Siri to play music in a few different ways, the simplest is to say "Play <track name>". You can also use commands such as "Play rock" and "Play my exercise playlist". Assuming you have some music defined as rock or a playlist called Exercise, they will start to play.

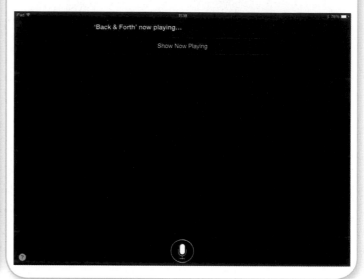

Finding an Email

As well as being able to search for things on the web, Siri lets you easily search for things on your phone. This includes notes, emails and messages. Ask Siri to "Find the email about iPad" and any emails containing iPad in the subject will be displayed.

Getting Directions

This feature is currently only available to US iPad users, but should be expanded to other countries, including the UK, soon. Direction requests can be phrased in a number of ways, from "How do I get home?" to "show me <address> on the map". You can also ask questions such as "Where is the nearest train station?".

Sending Messages

Once you get used to how you need to speak to Siri, sending messages using the assistant becomes easy and even fun. When dictating a message (or email, note, etc) you need to remember to speak the punctuation. To send a message, you can either say "Tell my wife I'll be home late" or "Send a message to John". In the latter case, Siri will then ask what you want the message to say.

Setting Reminders

You can use Siri to set both time-activated and location-activated reminders. You can say "Remind me about my meeting at 4pm" or "Remind me to buy milk when I leave work". Siri will then confirm the reminder and ask if it is correct. You then just say "yes" to set it.

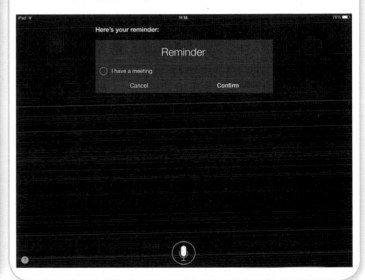

Sending an Email

Press and hold the Home Button to access Siri and ask to send an email to the name of one of your contacts (whose email address you have in your Contacts list). You will then be asked to add a title to your email. Next you dictate the content of your email. You will need to say the word "Comma" or "Full Stop" at the appropriate places. When you're finished simply tap the "Send" link or answer "yes" when asked if you want to send the email by Siri. You can stop this process by saying "Cancel".

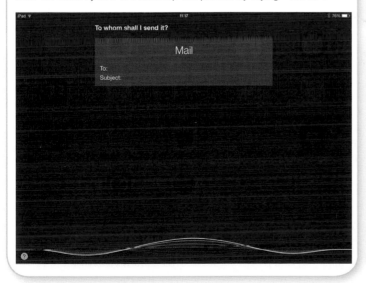

Sending a Text Message

Press and hold the Home Button to access Siri and ask to send a "message" to the name of one of your contacts. Next say what you want the text content of the message to be. You will need to say the words "Comma" or "Full Stop" to add basic punctuation. When complete simply tap the "Send" link or answer "yes" when asked if you want to send the text message or "Cancel" if not. If you answered positively your message will now be sent.

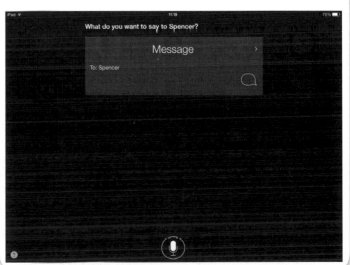

How to use iCloud

iCloud represents the future of data transfer and will revolutionise the way we use our devices, enabling our information and data to be accessed from any device, at any time.

 There are so many exciting apps available for the iPad it's virtually impossible to cover them all, and new ones are appearing all the time. However, one of the most exciting features of the new iPad operating system won't be immediately obvious because you don't have to download it. It's just going to be 'there'. Quite conveniently, that fits in well with Apple's mantra that accompanies its new range of apps to go along with iOS 7. The buzz phrase from Apple is 'It Just Works' and this specifically refers to the company's new data storage system known as iCloud. The term data storage doesn't do it justice though, because iCloud is much, much more than that.

The philosophy behind the software is based on the changing face of technology in the home, on the move and in business. In the past the home computer was the centre of everything. It's where music was downloaded, email was accessed, the Web was surfed and so on. With the advent of Internet phones, iPod touch and of course the iPad the computer's role has been diminished. We can now perform on our iPad most of the tasks for which we used to use our computer. The problem that this shift in balance has caused is that we now have information, apps, music, images and details spread across multiple devices, making it very difficult to keep track of everything. Manually connecting and syncing all your devices every time you make a change to something can be laborious and time consuming. Applications like Dropbox make things easier but it's still not a perfect solution. iCloud will remove all the difficulties of running your life across multiple devices and you won't even notice it, or at least not once you've started using it.

iCloud is built into the core apps that form the basis of iOS 7. These are Calendar, Mail, Contacts, the Appstore, iBooks, Photos, and iTunes. Each will run just as it does now except with iCloud functionality built in. This will appear in the form of an extra button in iTunes for example. Previously if you downloaded a track from the iTunes store onto your iPod touch and wanted to listen to it on your iPad, you'd have to sync it from your iPod touch to your computer and then sync the computer with your iPad. With iCloud, when you download a track to your computer or device, it's automatically downloaded to all your devices. In other words, if you download a track to your computer it will immediately appear in your iTunes playlist on your iPod touch..

The same goes for apps. Whichever device you download the app onto, it will automatically be downloaded to all your others. Calendar will be fully synced. Each time you make a new entry or edit an existing one the data

will be updated across all your devices keeping them all fully up to date. You can also share calendars so if for example your partner adds a date to your social diary on their device it will immediately appear on your own. iCloud is completely compatible with iWorks so if you're a regular user of Numbers, Pages or Keynote you'll be able to access, edit and show all your files on whichever of your devices you have to hand. All document changes are automatically saved and uploaded to iCloud so the documents are all updated simultaneously. That way all of your devices will always have the latest versions on them.

Photostream is the new images and videos app that makes sharing pictures and movies easier than ever before. Images are automatically shared in Photostream. It remembers the last 1000 images uploaded on each device, so if you want to keep particular images you'll need to move them into a different folder so they won't be automatically removed. This only applies to mobile devices. There's no limit to the number of images you can store in Photostream on your computer. In addition they're stored on the iCloud server for 30 days giving ample time to connect other devices so they can be downloaded.

Last but not least iCloud backs everything up once a day so you'll never lose any data. It's also incredibly handy if you get a new phone or device. All you have to do is enter your Apple ID and password and all your apps, music, settings and so on will be downloaded automatically.

To use iCloud all you need is an Apple ID. Everything is automatic. Once you're signed into your devices you don't have to worry about anything. All the operations take place automatically. All you need to do is carry on doing whatever you were doing. Finally, if you don't want to make use of iCloud for whatever reason, there's a simple on off switch in the Settings menu, but why anyone would want to turn it off we have no idea!

Summary:

To give it the most basic of descriptions, iCloud is a server that automatically updates and backs up all your apps, files, music and everything every time you download or update anything. You'll never have to worry about syncing your devices ever again because with iCloud it just happens without you having to lift a finger. In the future you'll wonder how you ever existed without it.

Signing up for iCloud

Linking your iPad to iCloud is very easy. Having initially set up your iPad via iTunes, or via a Wi-Fi connection using the PC Free set-up option, you will have reached the iCloud link screen. If you linked to iCloud at this point during set up please skip to the "Customising iCloud" feature on the next page. If not, then carry on reading and we'll take you through the process from start to finish.

Step 1   From the Settings app on your home screen, scroll down the options until you find the iCloud link, now tap it to move on.

Step 2   On this screen you will have to enter your Apple ID details or if you are a first time user sign up for an account via the "Get A Free Apple ID" link at the bottom of the screen.

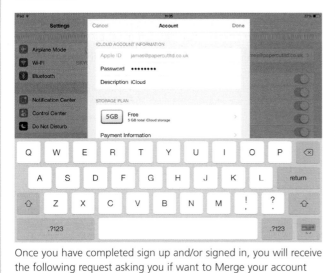

Once you have completed sign up and/or signed in, you will receive the following request asking you if want to Merge your account with iCloud, click the "Merge" link.

Step 3   You will now receive a second request. This one is a little more conventional and simply asks to confirm use of your locational service on your device. Make your selection to progress, a positive reply is not necessary but is suggested.

Step 4   From this page you can choose which file types and apps you wish to link to your iCloud account. Now, bear in mind that you do have a limitation placed upon your account of 5GB – additional space is available for an extra cost.

Step 5   Scroll down to the bottom of the page and click the Storage and Back up link to be taken to the following page. Here you can check your storage volumes and also choose to click the iCloud Backup option on.
This way any time you plug your iPad in to charge, or it is locked but connected to a Wi-Fi account it will automatically back up any new content to your iCloud account. If you wish to use this extremely useful ability slide the switch to the on position and agree to the bypassing iTunes back up pop up. You are now connected to iCloud.

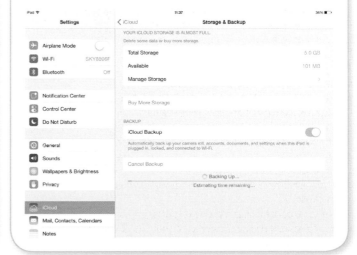

Customising iCloud

iCloud is a huge leap forward both in terms of data storage and how you manage the content on your iPad. iCloud links to a large array of iPad applications and although all of these links will prove exceptionally useful, you may want to only use the applications that will directly benefit you. For this guide we will take you through each stage of optimising your iCloud usage.

Step 1   From the home screen select the Settings option, scroll down to the iCloud link and tap it. On this page you can choose which content you wish to share over iCloud. Mail, Contacts, Calendars, Reminders, Safari Bookmarks and Notes are fairly straightforward.

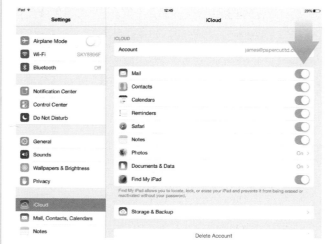

By checking the slider to the "On" position, all new content that is sent to or generated by these apps will be automatically uploaded to iCloud during sync.

Step 2   The Photo stream option is a little different as all images taken or downloaded via your iDevice will be uploaded to iCloud as usual but these images will be also be shared over all other iCloud linked devices on your network. This may cause problems due to the size of your images and the memory capacity of your other devices.

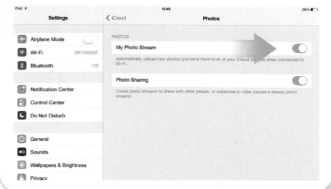

Step 3   If you choose to share through the Documents & Data option, all documents generated via your device or a host of applications will be uploaded to iCloud. This is very useful but we would suggest you keep a close eye on your iCloud data storage levels.

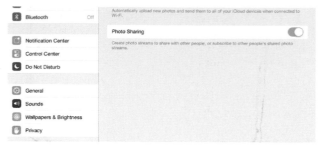

From this link you can also choose to upload said data via mobile data transfer; we advise you to check your data package with the network provider before selecting this link.

Step 4   The Storage & Back up link at the bottom of the page allows access to your iCloud account, so you can check how much storage you have left, or purchase more if needed.

Step 5   Also on this screen you can choose to use iCloud Backup option which enables you to sync directly with iCloud without needing to connect your iPad to the charger. By selecting this option you can automatically back up all new data in real time when the device is connected to your Wi-Fi network.

Shared Photo Streams

Photo Streams allow you to view images taken on an iPad, on your iPad, without having to physically transfer them across to the device. Shared Photo Streams allow you to easily create a gallery of images and share them with friends and family via iCloud, Apple TV or the web. People invited to view the photos can Like and comment on them.

Step 1 This feature is turned off by default, so the first thing you need to do is turn on Shared Photo Streams in the iCloud settings. You don't need to have Photo Stream turned on to use it.

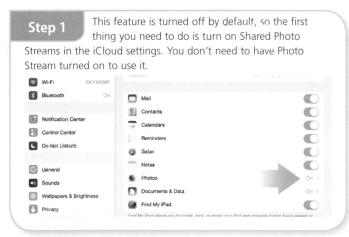

Step 2 Now open the Photos app and navigate to Shared Streams. To continue with this process tap the Shared Icon on the bottom of the screen.

Step 3 Give your shared photo stream a name and then tap the Next link, now you can add the people you wish to join the photo stream.

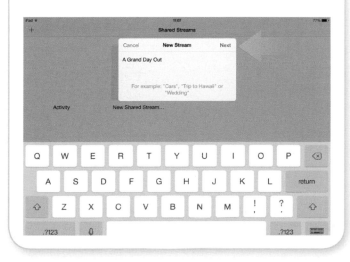

Step 4 You can you select the images you wish to add to the your Shared Stream from your Photos collection, or simply add a complete moment.

Step 5 You can now add a comment regarding your photos if you wish, and then you can post your images to your new Photo Stream. They will then be shared with your selected contacts.

Photo Comments and Notifications

If you are invited to start sharing a photo stream, you will be able to comment on and Like the images you see there. Once you have accepted the invitation to share, you will also receive notifications when new images are added to the shared stream (assuming you have notifications turned on in settings). If you are the one who shared the photo stream, you will receive notifications when someone Likes or comments on your photos.

How to use the FaceTime App

FaceTime enables real time video calling. With it you can communicate face to face with anyone else who has FaceTime installed on their Mac, iPhone, or iPad.

The FaceTime App's Key Features Explained

We've highlighted the key features of this application to help you understand better how it works.

You can check your camera and positioning via this small window.

This large area contains the view from your contact's selected camera.

To mute the sound simply tap here, to restore the sound tap here once again.

To end a FaceTime call just tap this button once.

To switch between the front facing and rear camera tap here.

What do I need to use FaceTime?

The video phone has been a staple of Sci-Fi movies since the birth of the genre. Over the years there have been many attempts to make video phones a reality, but none of them have ever caught on. As with so many other things though, Apple has taken the concept and made it work. FaceTime offers video chat on all your Apple devices, so let's give it a try. To use FaceTime all you'll need an Apple ID, an Internet connection and a contact who also has FaceTime on their Mac, iPhone, iPod or iPad.

How do I make a FaceTime Call?

Step 1 You can add contacts to your list and click on them to make a FaceTime call. You'll need either a phone number or an email address. You can stay signed in and available to take FaceTime calls at all times.

Step 2   Now select the contact from your list but instead of contacting them directly via their number, press the FaceTime link displayed below their number.

Step 3   You may have to wait a moment until the call is answered and then the chat can begin. Notice you will appear in the small window, while your contact appears in full screen.

Step 4   To end the call simply hit the large red "End" button at the bottom of the screen and you will be returned to the Contacts application.

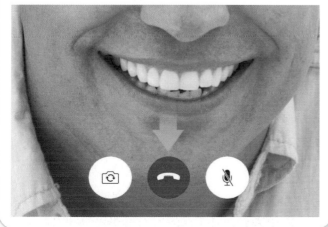

Turning off FaceTime

If you don't want people contacting you unexpectedly you can go into the Settings menu and then from this location turn FaceTime off by switching the slider to the Off position as shown here.

The Do Not Disturb Mode Explained...

Although a FaceTime visit from a family member or a dear friend can make your day, sometimes you may not be able to accept their call. For these times you can use the Do Not Disturb option from the main setting menu screen. To switch Do Not Disturb on simply move the slider to the "On" position. By doing this you will put your iPad into Do Not Disturb mode, meaning your iPad will automatically reject all incoming FaceTime calls.

You can customise your Do Not Disturb settings to enable calls from individuals or set out a time period each day where you require quiet time. To customise your FaceTime calls, open the settings menu and tap the Notifications option from the right side bar, then select the Do Not Disturb option at the top. You will now be greeted with this screen:

here you can schedule a time during which you can be reached. You can also select who can contact you at all times and finally allow repeated calls, which allows people to recall you within three minutes of their last call.

Making Your iPad Secure

For this feature we will take you through your various options to increase your iPad's security by setting up stronger passwords.

These short tutorials may help you make your iPad a little less attractive in the eyes of a potential thief and at the very least offer you a little extra peace of mind.

Creating a More Secure Passcode

Although the simple four-digit passcode may be a deterrent to many wrongdoers, you can also choose to change your password to a massive 25 character code using any mix of digits, letters and characters.

Step 1 — Visit Setting options

To activate this longer passcode option you must first head to the Setting options and then select the General options.

Step 2 — Turn Simple Passcode off

From this screen move the Simple Passcode slider to the off position, and re-enter your four digit passcode. Now you can enter your much longer passcode. You can use any mix of digits, letters and special characters, but a much easier option is to use a simple but memorable phrase of several long words. It's harder to crack and much easier to remember.

Step 3 — Re-Confirm Your Passcode

Re-confirm your passcode and it will be activated.

Keeping Your iPad Safe

Should the worst happen and your iPad is lost or taken without your permission, all may not be lost with a lot of help from Find My iPhone.

Find My iPhone is an important addition to iOS 7 and, ironically, your iPad. For the purpose of this feature we will take you through the entire set up process and walk you through a lost device scenario. We sincerely hope that you never have to use any of the following but it is better to be fore-armed should the very worst happen.

Initial Set-Up and Activation iPad Set-Up

During initial set-up, you can choose to install and use the Find My iPhone application and the pre-loaded app will be available from your home screen. Alternatively you can also download the app directly from the App Store.

Step 1   *Activating Find My iPhone*

Before you can move on you will need to confirm that you have activated Find My iPhone from the iCloud options page from the Settings menu.

Step 2   *Log in to Find My iPhone*

Tap the Find My iPhone application and you will be taken to this log in screen.

Step 3   *Entering Your Apple ID*

Enter your Apple ID and password and you will be signed into the application.

Step 4   *Linking Your Apple Devices*

On this screen you will see all iDevices that have been linked to your Apple ID. A green display to the left of the name indicates the device is traceable via your iPhone.

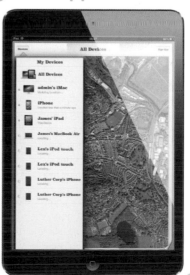

Setting Up Find My iPhone on a Desktop Computer

For peace of mind we would advise you to set up Find My iPhone on your desktop computer, thus enabling you to track any of your devices should you find yourself unable to access your iPad.

Step 1 — *Accessing iCloud from your computer*

From your desktop computer access the Internet and visit: *www.icloud.com*

Step 2 — *Enter your Apple ID*

Enter your Apple ID and password and you will be taken to the hub screen.

Step 3 — *Click Find my iPhone*

Ignoring the other options for a moment click the "Find My iPhone" link from the on-screen options and re-enter your Apple ID password.

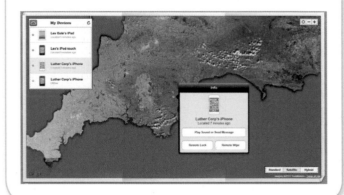

On this screen you will also see all iDevices that have been linked to your Apple ID, once again a green display to the left of their name indicates the device is traceable via www.icloud.com.

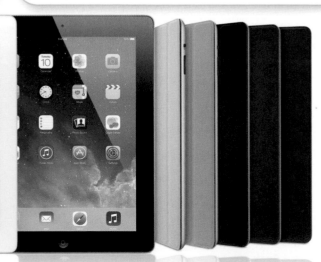

Using the iPad's
Lost Mode

You can stay in touch with a lost iPad by using this fantastic app, which could also help you in getting your iPad returned.

Step 1
You obviously need to have the Find My iPhone feature set up and enabled to use Lost Mode. To do this, open Settings > iCloud > Find my iPhone and turn on the service. You will need to sign in using your Apple id.

Step 2
In the event that you lose your iPad, log in to https://www.Icloud.com/#find and wait until your device is shown on the map. Click on your device and you will see several options, including Turn on Lost Mode.

Step 3
Click on the Lost Mode option and you will be prompted to lock your missing iPad with a 4-digit code. This code will allow you to unlock the device when you get it back, so make sure you use a code you will remember.

Step 4
The next thing to do is to add a phone number that you can be contacted on. This displays on the lock screen of the iPad and will mean the finder can contact you to arrange its return to you.

Step 5
Finally, you will be asked to write a short message to whoever finds the iPad. There will be a simple pre-written message in place for you to use, or you can write your own. Keep it short and to the point.

Step 6
The iPad will now be locked. Anyone finding your beloved device and trying to activate it will see your message and the phone number you included. Remember that you can continue to track the iPad as long as it has a Wi-Fi or 3G connection.

Share Files
Using AirDrop

The AirDrop feature is an addition to the iOS that makes sharing files and links far easier than ever before.

With this feature, all iOS and Mac OS X Maverick users will be able to send files over wireless Bluetooth networks, both quickly and securely. In this guide we will show you how to get the most from the excellent AirDrop.

Step 1 Before you attempt to use AirDrop you will need to confirm that the Bluetooth function has been activated on both devices and the devices have been paired. Open the Control Center by using an upward swipe motion on the home screen, then tap on the AirDrop link to open your sharing options.

Step 2 You can select to turn AirDrop off, sharing only with contacts or sharing with everyone. The latter option will require you to accept any shared files, thus maintaining security.

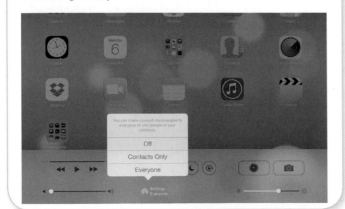

Step 3 Now select the file you wish to share, whether it's an image, a Safari link or a document, and then tap the AirDrop option and choose your recipient from those available.

Step 4 When you are being sent a file using AirDrop, you will see this screen. Here you can either Accept or Decline downloading the file. When you have accepted and downloaded the file it will be accessible from its host application. Safari links will open via Safari, photos via the Photos app and so on.

Add Effects To Your Photos

Photo Booth is great fun, enabling you to add all kinds of crazy effects and distortions to photos in real time as you take them.

The Photo Booth App's Key Features Explained

We've highlighted the key features of this application to help you understand better how it works.

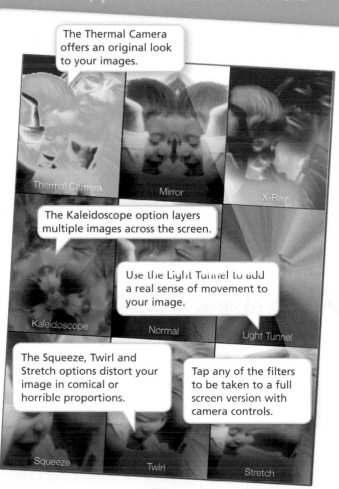

The Thermal Camera offers an original look to your images.

The Kaleidoscope option layers multiple images across the screen.

Use the Light Tunnel to add a real sense of movement to your image.

The Squeeze, Twirl and Stretch options distort your image in comical or horrible proportions.

Tap any of the filters to be taken to a full screen version with camera controls.

What do I do?

Open the app and angle your iPad so you can see yourself in the screen display. Tap the Effect button and you'll be presented with various effects that can be applied to the image.

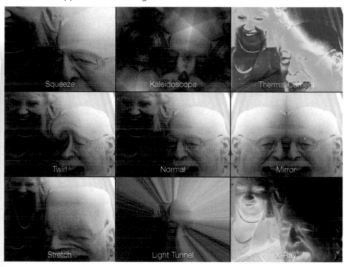

You can move your head around to see the effect better and some effects can be further distorted by dragging parts of the image with your finger. When you get a pose you like, take a snap by tapping the camera icon. Your Facebook profile will never be the same again!

Where are the images saved?

Your Photo Booth images will be saved in the album titled Camera Roll in Photos on your iPad.

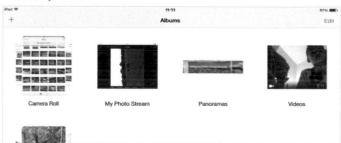

How to Edit
Photos on Your iPad

iPhoto is a new addtion to the iLife collection of iOS apps and gives you a great way to not only organise and display your photos, but also edit, improve and correct them. Using only your fingers, you can make a blue sky bluer, a landscape greener or a smile brighter.

Getting images into iPhoto

Beaming
If you are importing photos from a iPhone or iPod which also has iPhoto installed, you can use wireless beaming to copy the images over at full resolution. If transferring a lot of photos, this can take some time.

Sync
You can sync photos from your Mac or PC to the iPad using iTunes. You will need to sync to the Photos app, but any images in that app will also appear in iPhoto.

Email or SMS
You can save any images attached to emails or SMS messages to the Camera Roll. The Camera Roll images will automatically be available in iPhoto.

Update to iOS 7
If you haven't already, you should make sure that your iPad system software is updated to the latest version. Aside from numerous general updates and goodies, 7 gives you the ability to delete Photo Stream photos, adds a new camera app and is required for the newest versions of the iLife apps (iPhoto, iMovie, etc).

Camera Connection Kit
If you have the Camera Connection Kit adaptors, you can easily import images directly from a digital camera or from an SD card. Images imported in this way are at full resolution.

Photo Stream
Using iCloud, you can automatically push all images to all of your devices. Photos taken on your iPhone will automatically appear in a folder in iPhoto.

Beam photos to your iPad

As long as two iOS devices have iPhoto installed, you can wirelessly beam photos between them. Photos transferred in this way remain at full resolution. For this guide we are going to look at beaming from iPhone 4s to iPad 2, but the same steps apply for any iOS 7 device.

Step 1 Open iPhoto on both devices. Tap the Settings icon (cog) and turn on Wireless Beaming and Include Photo Location. Also make sure that Location Services are turned on the main iOS settings.

Step 2 On the sending device (the iPhone in this case), select a photo, album or event and tap the Send > Beam. You can then select all photos in an album or event, or you can select individual images.

Step 3 Wait for iPhoto to detect the iPad on the wireless network and then tap Beam Photos. Beaming a large number of photos can take a while, and if either device goes into sleep mode the process will be aborted.

Step 4 On the receiving device (the iPad) you will see a notification asking you to accept the beamed photos. Tap Yes. If you beam an edited photo, the original and the edited photo will appear in the beamed album.

Viewing photos

There are four different ways to view the images in iPhoto, controlled using the four tabs at the top of the main screen.

Albums

This shows any albums uploaded using Photo Stream, created in the Photos app or synced from iTunes. Any photos you take with the iPad camera are automatically put into an album called Camera Roll. As soon as you edit any image in iPhoto, the app creates another new album called Edited where it keeps a copy of the edited image.

Photos

This will show all of the individual photos on the iPad, including screenshots and edited images.

Journals

Journals are collections of images of your choice, put together on a choice of backgrounds. Perhaps your favourite photos from your last holiday or family event. You can also add notes, calendar pages, maps and more to your journals.

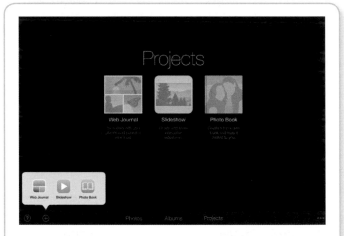

Events

Events shows groups of photos created on your Mac or PC and imported through iTunes, or groups of photos imported from a digital camera using the Camera Connection Kit.

Set Key Photo

You can choose the photo you want to show on the front of any user created album or event folder (you can't choose the key photo on albums created by iPhoto automatically). To set the key photo, open the album or event and then open the photo you want to use. Tap Edit and then the Settings icon at the bottom corner. From the pop-up menu, choose Set as Key Photo.

Deleting Photos

Many of the photos you see in iPhoto aren't actually stored in the app itself. iPhoto simply gathers all the photos on your iPad and displays them in one place ready to be edited. To delete photos from albums you have created, open the Photos app and delete either the album or individual images from there. Photos and videos synced from iTunes can be removed from iPhoto by connecting the iPad to your computer and deselecting the photos you want to remove. When you sync, the deselected images will be removed from iPhoto.

Editing photos

iPhoto allows you to quickly and easily edit your photos, from fixing red-eye in portraits to adding effects such as Vintage and Duotone. Edited photos have a small toolbox icon on them in the album or photo views.

1 Crop and Straighten
Allows you to crop images to a smaller size and straighten the angle of the framing.

2 Adjust Exposure
Opens controls for adjusting dark areas, light areas, contrast and brightness to compensate for specific lighting conditions in a photograph.

3 Adjust Colour
Allows you to adjust different colour elements such as skin tones, greenery and blue skies. You can also adjust the overall colour saturation.

4 Brushes
Several brushes that let you adjust and edit specific elements of the photograph. Brushes include Repair, Red-Eye, Lighten, Darken and Soften.

5 Add Effects
Adds a variety of effects to your image.Once an effect is chosen it can often be adjusted by sliding your finger across the small image in the tool bar.

6 Auto Enhance
A useful way to automatically enhance a photo.

7 Rotate Image
Rotates the image clockwise.

8 Flag Image
Flagged images appear in a separate album.

9 Favourite
Adds the image to a Favourites album.

10 Hide Photo
You can use this to hide photos you don't want to appear in iPhoto.

11 Next/Last Photo
Opens the next or last image in the list.

12 Settings
Settings change depending on what you are doing. Each of the main editing options has its own settings.

Maintaining Your
iPad's Battery

Because the battery of your iPad is not easily replaceable, it is essential that you follow certain steps to make sure that the battery has the longest possible usable life.

Replacing the iPad Battery

As with every Apple portable device (iPhone, iPod, etc), the iPad features an inaccessible battery. This means that you cannot just whip the back off and swap the battery for a replacement yourself. When the battery needs replacing (and all rechargeable batteries have a finite lifespan), you will need to send the iPad to a Authorised Apple Sevice Provider to have the work done. Unless you are an electronics whizz, trying to replace the battery yourself is a very bad idea, even if you can find a replacement battery pack.

Charging the iPad Battery

You can see the current battery power level by looking at the battery icon at the top right corner of the screen. You will also get a warning message when the battery power goes below a certain point. The mains power adaptor charges the iPad faster than using the USB to plug into your PC. As with anything that uses a rechargeable battery, it is a good idea to perform a full charge whenever possible, rather than performing lots of small charges.

27% Charged

Increase Your iPad Battery Life Tips

There are several tricks you can employ to make your battery last longer between each charge. Squeezing every possible drop of power out of the battery is something any iPad user will probably be familiar with.

One of the easiest ways to increase the battery life is to make sure that services like Wi-Fi and Bluetooth are turned off when you don't need them. In a perfect world you could have all your connections open all the time and not have to worry about them draining the battery. In the real world, however, things like Wi-Fi will drain the battery pretty quickly. You should also review your screen settings to see if the brightness can be lowered a bit, as this will also help the battery to last longer. What follows is our breakdown of some great tips that will help save your battery life.

Reducing Screen Brightness

Around the office we tend to keep our iPads' screen brightness under the 40% mark as this appears to be the best level for optimal battery performance. Avoid using auto brightness although you may need to raise the brightness levels when using your iPad in direct sunlight.

Manually Fetching Email

You can set your iPad to automatically collect your new email at pre-set times via the Settings menu. To do this your iPad will connect to your data provider, which uses battery power. To avoid this, select the manual setting and check your mail yourself when you are able.

Disabling Location Services

If you activate the Location Services your iPad apps are given access your device's GPS tools to provide location-based results. By doing this you are using both your Internet connection and GPS. Both are a drain on the battery, so turn them off.

Disabling Push Notifications

Numerous applications on the iPad, from pre-installed apps such as Mail to countless downloads from the App Store, give you the option to receive their push notifications. These do require an Internet connection to work, so take care to only enable access to key apps.

Closing all Background Apps

Although some argue against this, we have found that having apps that run in the background can be a drain on the battery. By closing recently run applications you could help maintain your battery life for a little longer than if you choose to run them.

Enabling a Shorter Auto-Lock Time

Your iPad will automatically lock itself if it has been left idle after a set period of time, and obviously the shorter this time the better it is for your battery. We would advise you to set your iPad to automatically lock itself after two minutes.

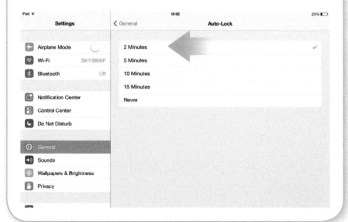

Updating iOS on Your iPad

Keeping your iPad updated with the latest version of the iOS operating system helps to keep your personal data safe and secure, and your tablet running smoothly.

Step 1 Having opened the Settings application, tap the second option from the top of the right bar, Software Update.

Step 2 If a new update is ready to download you will instantly see the iOS details window shown here. To download the update tap the link at the bottom of the screen. If no update is available your iPad will confirm your iOS is up to date.

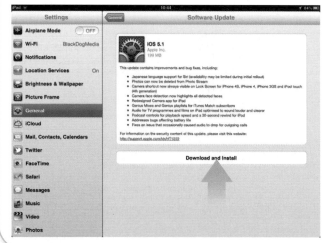

Step 3 Before updating your iOS you will need to agree to Apple's terms and conditions by pressing the "Accept" link on the top right of this pop-up.

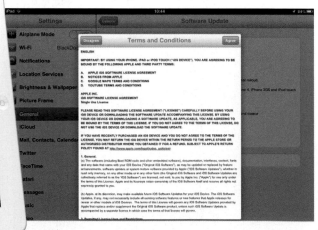

Step 4

Another pop-up will now appear recommending that you connect your new iPad to an external power source while updating. Although you can continue on battery power, it's still a good idea to plug in your charger.

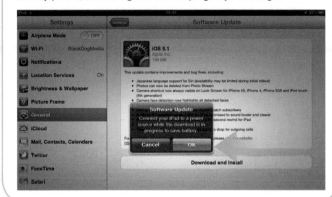

Step 5

Once the download begins an on-screen progress bar will appear giving you an estimated length of time required before the download is complete.

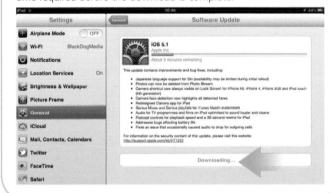

Step 6

Once the update has been downloaded it will automatically start to install once you have confirmed you are happy to update your iOS.

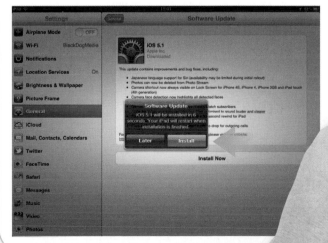

Step 7

The iPad will verify the complete download and then the installation process will begin, when this install is complete the iPad will automatically restart.

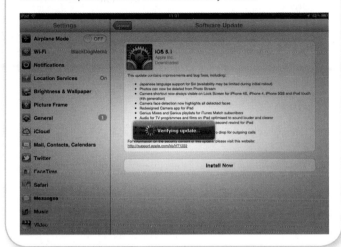

Step 8

Having restarted your new iPad is fully updated and ready for use.

Updating iOS
Using iTunes

Keeping your iPad up to date with the latest version of iOS is important. Each new version of the operating system adds new features and might also include fixes for known problems. Luckily, updating iOS is easy when you know how.

Step 1 Before you update your iOS device, it is a good idea to make a back up and sync all of your data. Connect your device to your PC or MAC using the USB data cable and open iTunes. In the left hand column, right click on your device and select Back Up from the menu. Wait for the back up to complete.

Step 2 To start the update process, select your device from the left hand column and on the screen that opens, under the Version heading, you will see an Update button. Click this to begin the update.

Step 3 If you haven't set iTunes to automatically check for updates, you will see a message asking you if you want to manually check now. You can change this setting in Preferences later if you wish.

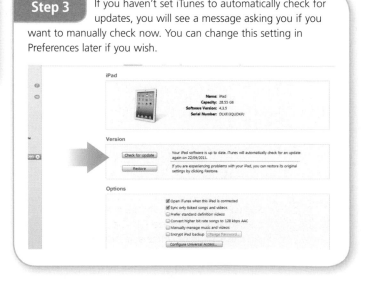

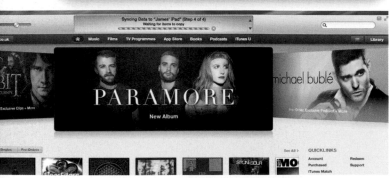

Step 4   If you didn't sync your device before starting the update process, you will then be asked if you wish to do it now. Syncing stores all of the data (music, apps, files, etc) in the iTunes library, so if the update fails to complete for any reason, your data is safe.

Step 5   Now that your data is safe, you can continue with the update. You will be shown information about the latest update, including all new features it adds and any bug fixes it will apply to your device. This screen will also show which devices are compatible with the current update.

Step 6   The next thing you will need to do is agree with the Software License Agreement.

Step 7   You will now need to wait for the update to download onto your device. The time this takes can vary, so go and make a cup of coffee and check back in 30 minutes.

Step 8   Don't disconnect your USB cable during the update. It is also a good idea not to use your computer for anything else while the update process is underway. Your device may disconnect and reconnect itself whilst updating, so don't worry if you see disconnect pop-ups.

Step 9   When the process is complete, you can check to see which version is installed by selecting your device from the left hand column and clicking on Summary. The software version will be shown near the top of the screen.

Restore from Back Up   If anything goes wrong (don't worry, it rarely does), you can restore your device to its previous state easily. Plug in your device and right click on it in the left hand column of iTunes. Choose Restore from Back Up and follow the steps detailed.

7 Changing Your iPad Wallpaper

You are able to set a custom wallpaper on your iPad, either from one of your own pictures, or from any website gallery you've found using Safari.

Step 1 When you have found an image using Safari press and hold on the screen to get the "Save Image" option to appear. Or you can use an image from your Photo Library.

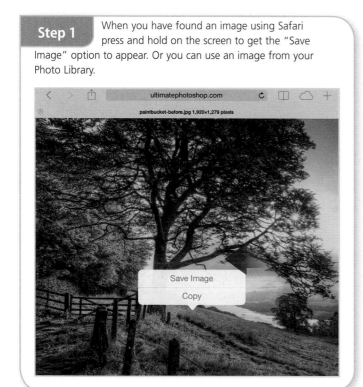

Step 2 Go back to your Home Screen and select Settings > Brightness & Wallpaper.

Step 3 Flick right and select Camera Roll, then select the image you saved.

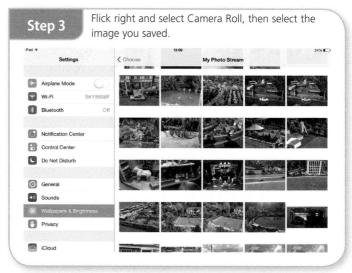

Step 4 Choose either the Set Lock Screen or Set Home Screen or both to make it your wallpaper.

How to use the iPad's Split Keyboard

Typing on the standard on-screen keyboard can be tricky if you're using your iPad in the upright (portrait) position. Either you have to type one-handed or just use your thumbs, which can involve some uncomfortable stretching to reach the middle of the keyboard. Since the launch of iOS 5 this is no longer a problem, because you can split the keyboard into two thumb-friendly halves using a simple on-screen gesture. What follows is a short guide to doing this, making every use of the upright position keyboard, whether sending emails or web browsing, far easier.

Open any application that requires use of the portrait positioned keyboard, for example the Notes app as seen here, then using your thumbs - placed closely together - press down on the keyboard.

Now quickly move your thumbs apart without removing them from the screen and it will split into two, allowing you to thumb type whilst holding the iPad.

Reverse the above process to return the keyboard to the normal full screen display.

How to Force Restart Your iPad

This brief tutorial will explain how to force your iPad to restart in the unlikely event that it freezes up. Don't worry, forcing your iPad to restart will not cause any loss of data, with the possible exception of any unsaved work you were doing when it crashed.

Step 1 It's actually very easy, once you know how to do it. Click and hold down the Sleep/Wake button (located on the upper-right corner of your iPad). While you're holding down the Sleep/Wake button, hold down the Home button as well (located on the front of your iPad at the bottom).

Step 2 Hold down both buttons until your iPad powers off. It will reboot and start again with a small silver Apple image on the screen. It takes about 30 seconds for the iPad to completely start up.

7 How to use Bluetooth

The Bluetooth function on your iPad allows you to use lots of different peripherals such as keyboards and headphones. Before you can use these wireless extras, you will need to pair them to your iPad.

Step 1 Follow the instructions given with your chosen Bluetooth peripheral to make it visible to your iPad. The actual steps needed to do this vary between devices so make sure to follow them carefully.

Step 2 Make sure that Bluetooth on your iPad is turned on. To do this, go to Settings > General > Bluetooth and tap the button to turn Bluetooth on.

Step 3 You will now need to select your device from the list. You might need to enter a PIN depending on what device you are trying to pair. If a PIN is required, it will be supplied with the Bluetooth device.

The name of the paired device will appear on screen along with an icon showing you what type of device you are paired with (headphones, keyboards, etc). If you're using a Bluetooth keyboard and you want to switch back to using the virtual keyboard, simply turn off Bluetooth. If the keyboard has one, you can also press the Eject key. The device will still be paired with your iPad.

Unpairing a Bluetooth Device

If you want to change to a different Bluetooth device, you will first need to unpair your iPad from the previous one.

Step 1 Open the main Settings, open the General settings page and then select Bluetooth. You will need to turn Bluetooth on if it isn't already.

Step 2 Choose the device you want to unpair from the list, select it and touch Forget This Device. You can now choose a different device to pair with.

The Bluetooth icon which appears at the top of the screen lets you instantly see if you are paired with a device or not. If the icon is white, that means Bluetooth is on and paired to a device. If the icon is grey, Bluetooth is on, but no devices are paired with your iPad.

Gesture Controls
for Your iPad

Get the most out of your iPad's amazingly responsive touch-sensitive screen by mastering the special gestures that control it.

The Switching Between Apps

Place four fingers at the right side of the iPad screen. Now quickly move your fingertips towards the left.

Using the Pinch to Home Screen

Place all five fingers in a open palm position on the iPad screen Close your fingers until they meet and the app will close.

Revealing the Multi-tasking Bar

Place four fingers at the bottom of the iPad screen. Now quickly move your fingertips towards the top of the screen.

iPad User Help, Problem Solving Tutorials & Tips

Luckily for us iPad users, Apple has a long history of creating devices that are solid and reliable. That said, every piece of technology has its minor problems and annoyances, and the iPad (from the original, right through to the latest version) is no exception. Thankfully, few of the iPad problems or errors are terminal and, with a little bit of tinkering, most can be solved by the average user.

Troubleshooting Hardware

Your iPad, with reasonably sensible handling, should easily withstand a lot of use. It is, however, sometimes easy to see a hardware fault when it is actually software that is causing the problem. Here are some potential hardware problems and how to diagnose and hopefully fix them.

Restarting the iPad

Let's start with the basics! If you are noticing minor problems with your iPad (apps closing for no reason, button lag, etc.) you should try restarting it before you try anything else. To restart the iPad, hold down the Sleep/Wake button until the red slider appears and then use this to turn the tablet off. Wait for 30 seconds and then press and hold the Sleep/Wake button to turn the iPad back on.

Resetting the iPad

If the problem continues, you can try resetting the iPad instead of simply restarting it. Resetting is more drastic than restarting and should only be done if the previous option doesn't work. Resetting can, in some cases, cause data to be lost. To reset the iPad, press and hold the Sleep/Wake button and the Home button at the same time. Keep them both held for at least 10 seconds, when the Apple logo will appear and the iPad will reset.

Sleep/Wake Button

If the Sleep/Wake button does not seem to be working as it should (waking the iPad when pressed, etc), you should first try resetting the iPad. Press and hold the Sleep/Wake button for a few seconds until a red slider appears, and then slide the slider. Now press and hold the Sleep/Wake button until the Apple logo appears.

Fix Home Button Lag

As the only physical button on the front of your iPhone or iPad, the Home button gets used a lot during a normal day. Not only does the button return you to the home screen, but with the iOS update, it is now also used to access the multitasking screen (double click). Most of the time, you will find the button responsive, but there can be times when it lags or even needs a couple of presses before it responds. Before you start to panic and send your device away to Apple to be repaired, it is certainly worth trying a couple of easy fixes to see if they solve the problem.

iPad Power Issue Fix

We have found that if your iPad won't power on - and the screen stays completely blank without displaying the charging needed icon when you press the Home Button - there is no immediate need to panic. This has happened to us several times while using various iPad models, and there is a simple solution to fix it. Although we are not entirely sure why this happens, we have

managed to solve this issue by simply attaching the iPad to a charger and leaving it on charge for several hours. By doing so your iPad will ultimately spring back to life and will restart on its own accord. We cannot stress enough the importance of keeping your iPad charged and not letting the battery run out completely.

Fix 2 - Reboot the Device

The average iPad, iPhone or iPod stays on for hundreds of hours, only going into standby or sleep mode rather than actually shutting down and being rebooted. Most of the time this is fine and shouldn't cause any problems, but occasionally problems can build up and result in system lag or unwanted behaviour. It is a good idea to periodically reboot your device. You might be surprised just how many small problems and errors this simple action can fix.

Troubleshooting Apps

There are several possible reasons why your favourite app has started to misbehave or even stop working altogether. In most cases the problem is not terminal and can be fixed by one of the following methods.

Force Apps to Close

If a particular app is playing up, you can force it to close (and hopefully reset itself) in a couple of different ways. The first and easiest way is to double click the Home button, find the app in the Multitasking panel that opens at the bottom of the screen and hold your finger on it until it starts to jiggle. Tap the delete icon that appears in the top corner to close the app.

The second way to force an app to close, which is often useful if the app has frozen the screen, is to press and hold the Sleep/Wake button until the red slider appears. Then press and hold the Home button until the app closes.

Restarting the iPad

To restart the iPad, first turn it off by pressing and holding the Sleep/Wake button until a red slider appears. Slide your finger across the slider and the iPad will turn off after a few moments. Now turn your iPad back on by pressing and holding the Sleep/Wake button until the Apple logo appears.

Report App

If you are still encountering an issue with the app, you can use the App Store to report your problem. Open the App Store on iPad and locate the app. Scroll down and tap "Report a Problem." Select your issue and add any additional comments. Tap "Report" to submit your issue to the app developers.

Remove the App

If you are having issues with a particular app, try removing the app from your iPad and then reinstalling it.

Step 1 To avoid losing any app data, first back up your information.

Step 2 Touch and hold any app icon on the Home screen until the icons start to wiggle.

Step 3 Tap the "x" in the corner of the app you want to remove. You may be prompted to rate the app.

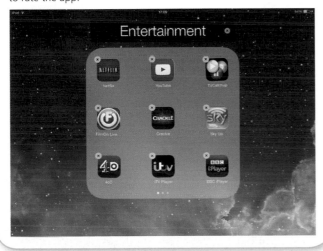

Step 4 Tap Delete to remove the app and all of its data from your iPad.

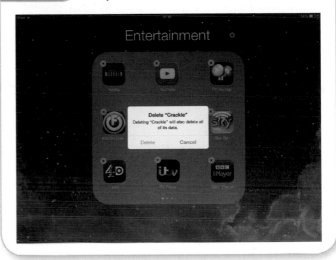

Step 5 Click the Home button to cancel or stop deleting apps.

Reinstalling an App

After removing an app from your iPad, use these steps to reinstall it. Open the App Store on your iPad and locate the app to reinstall. If you previously purchased the app, tap Purchased to find it quickly, then tap the download button. If prompted, enter your iTunes Store account information.

After the app is installed, check to see if your issue is resolved.

Troubleshooting Internet Connections on Your iPad

Having trouble sending an email? Struggling to get your iPad to connect to the Internet? Here is a step-by-step guide to troubleshooting connection issues. The tips referring to mobile data, carriers or SIM cards only apply to iPads with 3G capabilities.

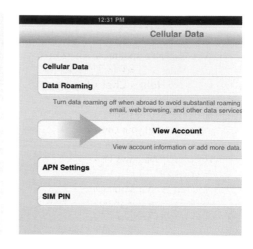

1. Check Your Signal

Check the status bar on your iPad to make sure you have a strong signal. If not, try changing your location or going outside. Make sure the iPad isn't in Airplane Mode. To turn off Airplane Mode, tap **Settings** > **Airplane Mode**. If you're not using Wi-Fi and you're trying to access the Internet, make sure you have a cellular data connection by checking next to the carrier name at the top of the screen (you should see 3G, E or O)

2. Reinsert Your SIM

Remove the SIM card by inserting the end of the SIM eject tool, or a small paper clip, into the hole on the SIM tray. Press firmly and push it straight in until the tray pops out. Gently remove the SIM card from the tray, make sure it is clean and then reposition the SIM card back in the tray. Return the SIM tray to iPad, then push firmly to fully reinsert.

3. Reset Network Settings

If none of the above solve the problem, you can try resetting your network settings. To reset your network settings, tap **Settings** > **General** > **Reset**, then scroll down and tap Reset Network Settings. Be aware that this will clear your current cellular and Wi-Fi network settings, including saved networks, Wi-Fi passwords, and VPN settings.

4. Check Carrier Service

If possible, call your data provider to check that there are no known issues with signal or service. They should also be able to tell you if you are in an area with little or no 3G network coverage.

5. Restore the iPad

Note: Restoring your iPad will result in all settings being reset, and all data and media wiped. If possible, sync fully with iTunes before restoring.

To restore your iPad, first make sure you are using the latest version of iTunes. Next, connect the iPad to the computer. In the left column under Devices, click on your iPad, then click on Restore in the Summary tab. Be patient while the process completes and don't be tempted to disconnect the iPad from the computer before being told it is safe to do so.

Troubleshooting and Problem Solving Issues with iTunes

Being able to connect to iTunes on your computer is an important part of making the most of your iPad. If you are having trouble connecting, try the following:

Update iTunes

Make sure you have the latest version of iTunes. To check for available updates of iTunes on a Mac, go to iTunes > Check for Updates. On Windows, go to **Help** > **Check for Updates**.

To install iTunes, you need one of the following operating systems on your computer:

- Mac OS X version 10.5.8 or later
- Windows 7; Windows Vista; or Windows XP
- If you are using a 64-bit version of Windows 7, be sure to download the 64-bit version of iTunes.

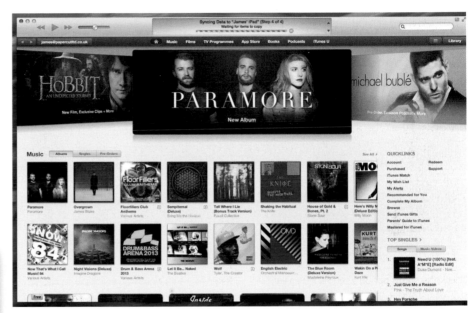

Check USB Connections

Try disconnecting and reconnecting the iPad. Whenever possible, always connect iPad to a USB port that is built into the computer instead of the keyboard or an external USB hub. If iPad still doesn't appear in iTunes, try a different USB port.

RESTART THE IPAD

To restart iPad, first turn it off by pressing and holding the Sleep/Wake button until a red slider appears. Slide your finger across the slider and iPad will turn off after a few moments. Next, turn iPad on by pressing and holding the Sleep/Wake button until the Apple logo appears.

If the iPad is not responding, press and hold the Sleep/Wake button and the Home button at the same time for at least 10 seconds, until the Apple logo appears. If your device does not turn on or displays a red battery icon, try recharging next.

RECHARGE THE IPAD

If the iPad is very low on power or if the battery is fully depleted, charge it using an AC adapter or connect to a high-power USB such as the one on your computer. If the iPad's battery is extremely low on power, the display may remain blank for up to two minutes before a low-battery image appears. If your iPad displays a low battery image, it can take up to 20 minutes of charging before the tablet will start up. You can press the Home button to check the current charging status.

Reinstall iTunes

In some rare instances, it may be necessary to remove all traces of iTunes, QuickTime, and related software components from your computer before reinstalling iTunes. For most technical issues though, reinstalling iTunes is an unnecessary and overused troubleshooting step. It is not necessary for Mac users to uninstall or reinstall iTunes.

iPad Apps Extras and Tips

Having discovered over the previous pages just how versatile your new iPad can be, we can now get down to the fun stuff; the Apps! Our team of Apple experts will share their choice of the best apps for keeping in touch, increasing productivity and keeping you entertained, apps you will use every day and so much more.

CONTENTS...

How to use the
App Store

Apps are the heart and soul of your iPad. There are thousands of them available from the App Store and they come in all shapes and sizes.

The App Store's Key Features Explained

We've highlighted the key features of this application to help you understand better how it works.

Focus your App Store search by selecting any of these four options.

Search titles and app descriptions for the entire App Store via this link.

In this area you will see the very latest apps that have been added to the App Store.

This window displays the latest recommended apps as chosen by Apple.

Click either of these five options to be taken to that area of the App Store.

Your Guide to the App Store

Apps are what the iPad is about. Whatever your lifestyle or interests, whether you use your device for work or play, you can't do anything without the right apps, and the place to get apps is the App Store.

Step 1   Tap once on the App Store icon to enter the App Store.

Step 2 The are six ways to search for apps on the App Store, the most obvious being the search bar on the top right corner. To use this feature simply tap the search bar and enter your search perimeters using the keyboard and hit search to see your results. Located next to the search bar are your App Store

quick links that take you to the key category links and the final More link which offers a quick link to each category of the App Store. Your other options are located at the bottom of the screen and they are: Featured, which are Apple's choice of the latest apps, Top Charts, the most popular paid and free apps, Near Me, uses your current location to provide you with apps that maybe of interest to you – tourist attractions, restaurants etc – and finally Purchased, a complete listing of all the apps you have downloaded through your Apple ID.

Step 3 Tap any app to see its info page. From here you can read a description, scroll through screenshots, tap on the ratings box to read reviews, send it to a friend from your contacts list or buy it for a friend.

Step 4 To purchase an app, tap the button with the price in it (or FREE if it's a free app). If it's a free app the button will change to **INSTALL** and for paid apps it will change to **BUY NOW**. Tap this and you'll be prompted to enter your Apple ID password. The app icon will then appear on your home screen with a progress dial to indicate how much longer the installation will take. When the progress dial disappears the app is installed and ready to use.

Step 5 Tap the More button to search for apps of a specific type. Scroll through the list of categories until you find the one you want then tap it to see the apps. The only exception to this is the Games category which brings up a sub menu of genre categories before you get to the games apps themselves. Each category can be sorted by top rated paid apps, top rated free apps and release dates using the buttons that appear at the top of the screen.

Step 6 Notice the three lines icon beside the More quick link at the top of the screen, this is your Wish List. Here you can add Apps that you have come across exploring the App Store that have tweaked your interest but are maybe a little too expensive or require some more research before you buy. You can add apps to your Wish List by tapping the top right share link on the apps page.

Step 7 Tapping Search brings up a text field. Tap this to access the keyboard and enter keywords or a specific app title to search the entire app store. Search results start to appear automatically as you type and if you see the one you want you can tap it to go straight to the app's screen.

Step 8 You can move about the App Store easily by using the search filters at the bottom of the screen or the cancel button that appears at the top left of the screen when available.

Step 9 When it comes to updating apps you can select the final option to the bottom right corner. Alternatively head back to the Setting menu and then tap the iTunes & App Store link. From here select the Updates option slider from the AUTOMATIC DOWNLOADS to the on position and your apps will update themselves.

Add More Apps to Your iPad Dock

Adding more or different apps to the app dock on your iPad is a good way to keep your most often used apps at your fingertips.

Step 1 Choose any of the apps on your home screens that you want to move to the dock and select it by touching and holding the icon until it starts to shake and a small X appears on the corner.

Step 2 With your finger still held on the app icon, drag it down the screen to the dock and position it where you want it to go.

Step 3 Your chosen app is now attached to the dock. You can add up to six apps to the iPad dock at one time. To remove an app from the dock, even one of the default ones, just hold your finger on it until it shakes and then drag it up onto the main home screen. Keeping your favourite apps in the dock means that they are always close to hand when you need them.

Close Running Apps
on Your iPad

After only a short time using your iPad, it is possible that you will have several apps running at once.

Step 1 You can quickly and easily bring up a list of currently running apps by double-clicking the Home button at the bottom of the iPad.

Step 2 On double-click, the app bar will slide up from the bottom of the screen and show icons for every app that is running. Touch and hold on any app you want to close.

Step 3 Any app that you have selected by touching the app screen can be deleted by simply flicking your finger in an onscreen upward swipe, causing the app to zoom off the top of the screen and close.

Step 4 Closing apps from the app bar just closes them. You don't have to worry that you are deleting apps. You can see how to delete apps elsewhere in these pages.

Step 5 You can repeat this process to close any of the apps shown on screen.

How to Rename
App Folders

You can create folders to contain your applications on your iPad to help keep your home screen tidy. Here is a quick guide to renaming previously created folders.

Step 1 Find the folder you want to rename and touch and hold the icon. The folder icon will start to shake showing you that it can be edited or moved. Tap the icon again while it is still shaking.

Step 2 This will open the edit bar. Click on the X at the end of the edit bar to begin editing.

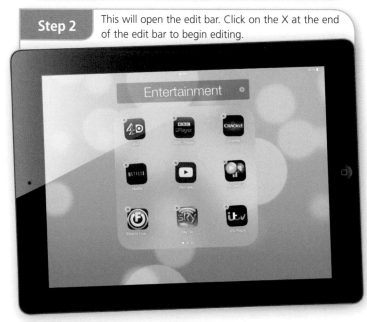

Step 3 Use the keyboard that pops up to change the name of the folder to whatever you want.

Step 4 Finally, press the Home button on your iPad to close the edit bar and display your folder with its new name.

Turn Off In-App Purchases on iPad

An increasing number of both free and paid apps include the ability to upgrade or add features from within the app itself via in-app purchasing.

Step 1 Open the main settings screen on your iPad and then click on General Settings on the left hand side of the screen. From General Settings, click on Restrictions.

Step 2 If this is the first time you have entered this screen, you will need to Enable Restrictions by touching the bar at the top of the screen. Doing this will prompt you to enter and confirm a 4-digit pin. Make this code something memorable but not too easy to guess by someone else.

Step 3 With restrictions enabled you will be able to change several settings which can help with the security of your iPad and apps. However, the one we are interested in for the moment is the option labelled In-App Purchases in the Allowed Content section. Turn this option off by touching the button and close the settings. In-app purchasing is now disabled on your iPad and cannot be turned on again unless someone knows your 4-digit pin.

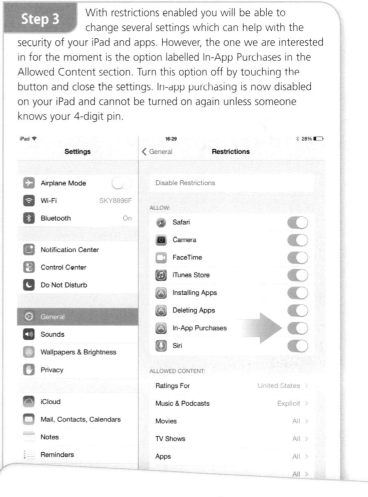

Permanently Delete
Unwanted Apps

Keeping your iPad clutter-free and running smoothly is important. Trying to use your iPad with app icons filling every home screen can be annoying.

Step 1 Open the Springboard and find the app you want to delete. You can delete any app you wish from this screen, just make sure you really want to be rid of it.

Step 2 Touch and hold the app icon for a few seconds until it starts to shake. In the corner of the app icon an X will also appear.

Step 3 Touch the X and you will be asked if you want to Delete the app, or cancel the action. Select Delete if you are sure.

Step 4 The app, including all data for it, has now been removed from your iPad.

Step 5 If iTunes is set to sync to your iPad automatically, and if the app is also stored in your iTunes account, you will need to remove it from there also. If you don't, iTunes will just reinstall it next time you connect. If you want to keep the app in iTunes in case you want it again at a later date, you can always just set iTunes not to auto-sync. The option for doing this is in **Edit > Preferences** found at the top of the main iTunes screen.

Easily Switch
Between Apps

Since the 4.3 update of iOS, your iPad has the ability to switch between several apps at once (multi-tasking). This means that you don't need to close your Facebook app if you want to, for example, check Twitter.

Step 1 To see which apps you have running, double-click on the Home button at the bottom of your iPad. You can do this whilst running any app.

Step 2 This shows all currently running apps. Tap the icon of the app you want to switch to.

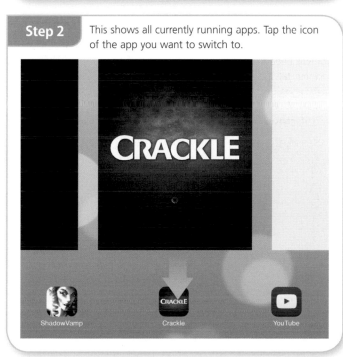

Step 3 If you have a lot of apps running, you might need to scroll the app bar to find the one you want. To do this, simply swipe your finger left or right across the app bar.

Step 4 You can have several apps running at once and can switch between them using this method, alternatively you can use a four finger right to left swipe to switch apps.

How to use the iTunes App

The iTunes store is the place to go for all your musical, audio, video and podcast needs. You can search music by genre, artist, song title and album title.

The iTunes App's Key Features Explained

We've highlighted the key features of this application to help you understand better how it works.

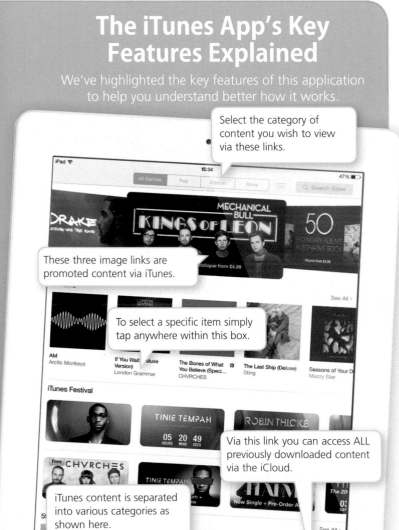

Select the category of content you wish to view via these links.

These three image links are promoted content via iTunes.

To select a specific item simply tap anywhere within this box.

Via this link you can access ALL previously downloaded content via the iCloud.

iTunes content is separated into various categories as shown here.

Where do I start?

The row of icons running along the bottom of the screen will take you to the section you require, be it movies, music, TV, podcasts or audiobooks. Click a category and you can start browsing with featured items and recommendations also appearing.

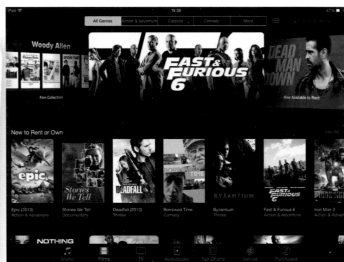

Buying movies & music

Click on Music or enter some keywords on the search field. Click on the matches and you'll have the option to listen to a sample, buy the album or buy individual tracks. This works in exactly the same way. The difference is in some cases you'll have the option to rent the movie. When you do this you have a limited time period in which to watch it before it's automatically wiped from your device.

Downloading Music and Videos through iTunes explained

You'll be so busy sending emails, browsing the Internet and posting on Facebook that you might easily forget that you are carrying around one of the most technically advanced multi-media devices currently available. You'll really be missing out if you don't take full advantage of the wealth of audio and visual entertainment that is available on iTunes.

Please Note: To access downloads from iTunes you must have a valid credit card linked to your Apple ID.

Step 1 Open the iTunes application from your Home Screen and enter your Apple ID via the Sign In link at the bottom of the home page.

Step 2 Search the iTunes store for your download or purchase via the Search bar link. This search covers all content from music to podcasts and the results will be categorised accordingly.

Step 3 Select the link to the download or purchase you have chosen and tap the Price or Install (if the download is free) button and then confirm you wish to continue.

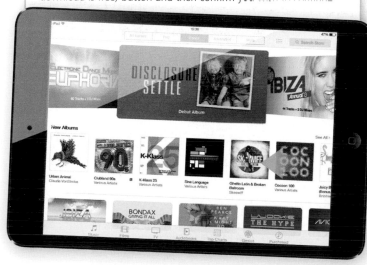

Step 4 While your selection is downloading you can either exit the iTunes store or continue to browse. The number of downloads currently running will be displayed in the bottom right corner.

Step 5 To view the time needed to complete running downloads tap the Download link at the bottom right to view a projected download time. This time is based upon the speed of your connection and the size of download.

Step 6 When completely downloaded you can access your file by exiting the iTunes app and opening the correct application. For audio files (Music and Audio Podcasts) open the Music app and for video files open the Videos app.

Remember to Sign Out

For safety reasons if you share your iPad with others it is best to sign out of iTunes after you have completed your session.

How to use the Music App

The Music app turns your iPad into a state-of-the-art musical entertainment suite which has all the great features you'll find on the latest iPod.

The Music App's Key Features Explained

We've highlighted the key features of this application to help you understand better how it works.

Your music collection is displayed via cover art in this area.

The track listing of the currently selected album is shown here.

Cycle through these options to change how your collection is viewed.

Listening to Your Music Collection

Having downloaded your favourite music to your iPad via iTunes you will want to enjoy it and this is how you, quite literally, bring music to your ears.

Step 1 Open the Music app from the home-screen and you will be greeted with several options: Store - click here to taken directly to iTunes. Playlists – Create your own soundtrack here. Artists – This option organises your music collection by the singer/band. Albums – Like the above although organised via album titles. Songs – an alphabetical listing of all the songs in your collection and the options to view your collection by Compilations, Composers or by Genre.

Step 2 For this short guide we have selected the Artists view, although this guide will work for all. You can now view all the artists available in your music collection. Tap the name of the one you wish to hear to be taken to a new screen.

Step 3 From this screen simply tap the name of the song you wish to listen to and you will instantly access your sweet music.

Notice the album cover and the information abut the song itself on the top bar. You can control the volume of the song, scrub to a certain point in the song using the bar under the title and skip back and forth between tracks using the double arrow buttons and play and pause the selected track using the triangle button.

Can I make my own Playlists?

Step 1 But of course! Open the Music app and tap the 'New' button, give your playlist a name and save it.

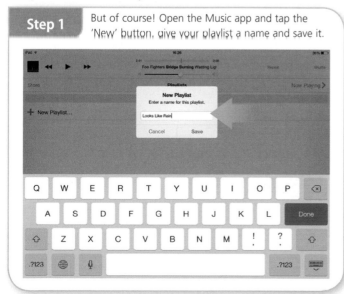

Step 2 You can then add tracks to it by tapping the 'plus' symbol next to them. You can also use Genius playlists to generate a playlist for you based on your personal tastes. Clever, eh!

How do I transfer music from my computer to my iPad?

Connect your iPad to the computer and open iTunes. From here you can choose to automatically sync all your music or to manually copy across selected tracks.

Do I need speakers to listen to music on my iPad?

No, you can plug in speakers or headphones if required but the iPad has built in audio output speakers as well.

How to use the Video App

With its amazingly sharp HD screen, the iPad is the perfect mobile platform for watching videos. So make the most of the Videos app and learn how your iPad can become your favourite place to watch movies and TV.

The Video App Explained

As the name suggests the Video app is your one stop shop for all of your big and small screen entertainment, this guide will show you how to see the big picture when it comes to using it.

Step 1 When you first open the Video app you will notice that it is empty, so your first port of call is to the Store link at the top left to do a little shopping. Flip back to the Using iTunes feature for more details on purchasing movies.

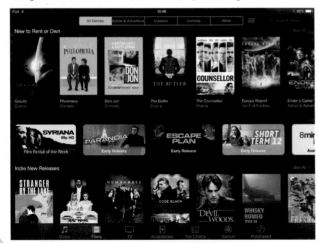

Step 2 Having downloaded your selection of movies, return to the home screen of your iPad and then tap the Video app, and you will see your choice of downloads displayed in their home category, accessed from the links at the top of the screen.

Step 3 You will notice that your video downloads are categorised in one of three areas; Movies, TV Shows and Music videos. To start viewing one of your videos, tap the image and you will be taken to the main screen. Next, tap the play icon in the top right.

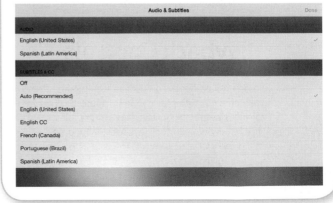

Step 4 Once you have started playback, you will have access to various controls. The volume is located in the bottom right, the scroll bar at the top of the screen allows you to adjust your playback position (see overleaf), play and pause are located in the centre of the bottom bar.

Step 5 Subtitles (if available) can be toggled on or off, or additional languages can be selected by tapping the icon to the lower right of the screen. From this icon you will also be able to change the language of the feature, should other tracks be available.

Step 6 If you are viewing a TV show which has multiple episodes, you can switch between them using the back and forth controls located next to the play/pause button. When you have finished watching you can return to the Video app by tapping the Done button.

Video Playback Controls

Having selected the video you wish to play as detailed above, your feature will begin and will be displayed in widescreen mode, which is essentially the same effect as turning the iPad to landscape. This will display almost all videos better, taking advantage of the full screen. Touching the screen at any time during playback will bring up the progress slider at the top and the control panel near the bottom. You can skip through the video by moving the progress slider by dragging your finger along it. All controls will disappear again after a few seconds if not being used.

Sharing Videos

As with apps and music, you can easily sync videos to your iPad from iCloud or iTunes. For iTunes connect your iPhone to your PC or Mac and wait for iTunes to open. If you have iTunes set not to auto-sync, you can choose which videos to sync to your iPhone from the left column. If you're using a Mac you can also sync videos from iPhoto. iTunes will also allow you to convert videos into a compatible format if the original won't sync. For iCloud syncing you must open the iTunes and App Store link from the Setting app and then move the slider for Music to the open position.

Watch iPad Videos on a TV

You can connect your iPad to most modern TVs using either Wi-Fi, an AV Cable or an iPad dock connector, and watch your videos on the big screen. This process is generally very simple: just plug in, browse to the correct AV channel on your TV and play the video on your iPad. You can also use Airplay if you have purchased the Apple TV device.

Renting Movies on Your iPad

In the iTunes Store you'll find movies to rent at a range of prices. Popular and new movies generally cost more to rent than older movies, but you

can find plenty of good films to watch for a really low price. You need to let your chosen movie download fully before you watch it (no streaming), but this shouldn't take too long if you have a decent connection. All rented movies will automatically delete themselves after a set amount of time. This time limit usually runs from the moment the movie starts to play, so make sure that you have enough time to watch your rented movie before you download and play it.

How to use the iBooks App

iBooks is a fantastic way to buy and read books. The app is free to download via the App Store, you can then browse a wide range of books from classics to best-sellers all in the built-in iBookstore.

Finding Books

When you download iBooks you get some free books with it to start enjoying the app, but to get more you can use the built-in iBookstore. To browse, you can pick a category such as; featured, top-selling, the New York Times Best-Seller, or browse by author, topic or title. If you find a book you like the look of, tap the cover to get additional information.

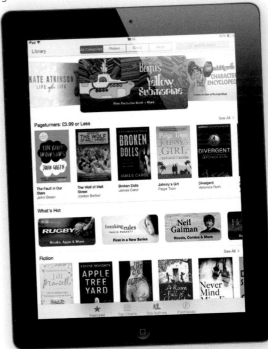

Downloading Books

In order to download the iBooks application and purchase a book from the iBookstore your iPad must have an Internet connection, as well as an iTunes store account. When you have downloaded the book you want, it will appear on the bookshelf of the iBooks app, all you need to do is tap it to begin reading. The iBooks App will automatically remember the last location of the book you were reading so no need to make a mental note. There are also a wide variety of display options for reading, even ones to help reading in low light.

Purchasing Books

Once you have found a book you like, you can buy it and download it to your iPad. There are some books, mostly old classics, which are free to download.

To purchase a book, find the book you want, tap on the price then tap Buy Now. Sign in to your iTunes Store account, then tap OK. This purchase will then be charged to your iTunes account. If

you want to download a book again, that you have already purchased, tap on purchases and find the book in question from the list. Then tap the download button to get it back onto your iPad. When books are downloaded to your iPad they are automatically synced with iTunes. If you ever sync your iPad with your computer and a book no longer appears on your iPad, it will automatically transfer over. This also acts as a form of backup in case you accidentally delete the book off your iPad.

iBooks 2 For Students

This app is perfect for students of all ages with its stunning interactive textbooks. Reference guides that spring to life with a tap or swipe of the screen, these guides offer a blend of easy navigation, easy highlighting and note-taking, searching and definitions and more. With further additions of lesson reviews and study cards, iBooks 2 app make learning more effective and more fun.

Now couple iBooks 2 with Apple's iTunes® U app and both educators and students will now have everything they need on their iPad, to learn, teach and take entire courses. iTunes U offers students free access to the world's largest catalogue of content which is currently used in the school curriculum. Learning made easy? Correct answer!

Syncing Books

You can use iTunes to sync books to your iPad. Once you have connected your iPad the Books Pane allows you to choose which books you want to sync. As well as the books you have downloaded via the iBookstore, you can download books in ePub format from many different websites and as long as they are DRM-free, they can also be placed onto your iPad to read. To add an ePub book, just download the book on your computer, then add it to your iTunes library. Connect the iPad to your computer, select the books you want to sync in the Books pane in iTunes, then sync your iPad.

Having a Book Read to You

If you are visually impaired, the iPad has a feature called Voice Over. This will make the iPad read a book aloud to you. Be aware there are some books that are not compatible with Voice Over.

Reading Books

Once you have a book on your iPad, tap on it to open it. To turn the pages, flick or tap near the edge of the page, this works on either side, in case you want to go back a page. When you have finished reading and decide to exit the book, iBooks will automatically remember where you were for next time. If you want to skip ahead to a different page further up the book, tap in the

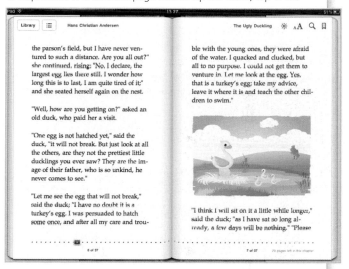

middle of the current page to bring up the controls that will appear at the bottom of the screen. Now drag the desired page number or chapter to where you want to go, then let go.

To get to the table of contents, just tap near the centre of the current page to show the controls, then tap on the Contents button.

From here you can tap on any of the content to jump straight to that section of the book, or you can tap on resume to go back to the page you were on.

Even though iBooks remembers where you left off when you closed the book, you are also able to set bookmarks. To do this tap and hold on and word on the page then select Bookmark. To remove the bookmark tap and hold the bookmarked word and tap delete. If you want to read your iBook lying down, make sure you use the screen rotation lock, as this will prevent it from switching between landscape or portrait when the iPad is tilted slightly.

How to use the Newsstand App

Newsstand is where you can buy, read and subscribe to your favourite publications directly on your iPad. Here's how it works and how you can get the most from it.

Downloading a Digital Magazine

Step 1 Tap the Newsstand icon to open Newsstand. If this is the first time you've opened Newsstand, all you'll see are a couple of empty shelves.

Step 2 To download magazines and other publications, tap the Store button to the top right above the shelves. This will take you straight to the Newsstand section of the App Store.

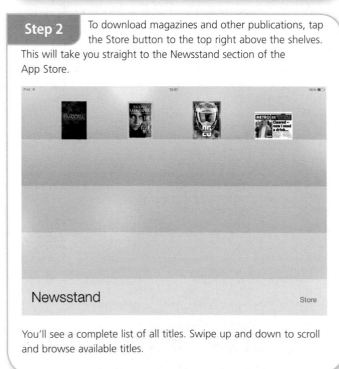

You'll see a complete list of all titles. Swipe up and down to scroll and browse available titles.

Step 3 You don't have to access the App Store via Newsstand to download new publications. All titles will still automatically download onto your virtual magazine shelf in Newsstand and you'll be returned to Newsstand when the download begins.

Step 4 All the publications you have downloaded are displayed on your shelves. To open a publication simply click on its cover. If you have more publications than can be displayed on the screen just swipe up and down to scroll between shelves.

Step 5 To rearrange the order of the publications on your shelves hold your finger over a cover – any one will do – until they all start to wobble. You can then drag each cover to the desired position. Press the Home button when you're satisfied.

Step 6 To delete a publication hold your finger on any cover until they all start to wobble. You'll notice a white cross in a circle has appeared next to each cover. Tap this and then tap Delete in the confirmation box that appears to remove the publication.

Buying Issues and Subscriptions

Having trouble seeing your Newsstand publications? Read on as we have the answers for you right here in black and white...

Step 1 Open your download, now to buy an issue or subscription, follow the in-app instructions. The interface varies from publisher to publisher and title to title.

Step 2 To read issues of publications you have purchased you'll need to follow the instructions within the appropriate app. As with purchasing, the interface varies between publications. Typically you'll find navigation buttons at the bottom of the screen but not always so be sure to follow all on-screen prompts.

Step 3 Change pages by swiping left to right. Pinch or tap to zoom depending on the publication and follow any further on-screen instructions to access additional features and functionality.

How to use the Kindle App

E-books have grown in popularity at an astonishing rate over the last few years, particularly in the US. With this massive uptake of e-books comes an equally large rise in sales of e-book readers (or e-readers). But while it is nice to have an e-reader with a six or seven inch screen, it isn't always practical to carry something that size around with you. Luckily, having an iPad means that you can have an e-reader in your pocket at all times.

Do I need another eBook reader?

By far the biggest and best-known supplier of e-books in the world is the mighty Amazon.com, which has its own amazingly good e-reader called Kindle. For tablets such as the iPad, Amazon has developed its own e-book reader app, which is also called Kindle. While there are many other e-book apps available including Apple's very own iBooks, there is no question that the Amazon Kindle is still the best around due to the extra titles this app can bring to your iPad. NOTE: You cannot purchase books directly from this app - you will need to visit your location's Amazon website and directly register an account with them.

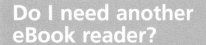

Setting up Kindle on Your iPad

This guide will show you how to install, set up and use this great free app on your iPad.

Step 1 Install Kindle. Kindle is free and available for download.

Step 2 Log in to Amazon via Safari. Once you have the app installed, open it and log in to your existing Amazon account. If you don't already have an account you will have to create one.

Step 3 Browse e-Books. Press the Menu button and choose either Cloud or Device from the lower menu. You will then see a list of e-book categories for you to browse directly from your Amazon Kindle account via the Cloud or books you have downloaded directly to your iPad. You can also search the store using the search field at the top of the screen.

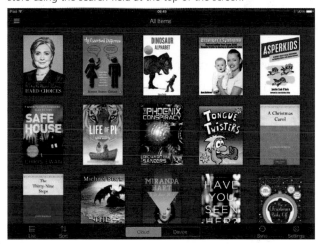

Step 4 To download an e-Book, you will need to visit the Amazon website via Safari and once you have found the book you want, click the Buy with 1 Click button. The payment will be taken from the card registered to your Amazon account.

Step 5 View a Sample. If you are not sure about the book you are viewing, you can choose to download a free sample section. Just click the Try a Sample button and it will download to the app home screen.

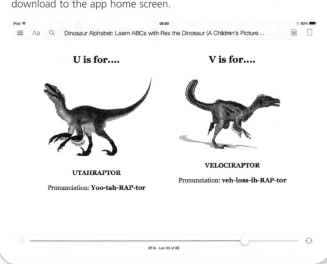

Step 6 Once your eBook has been purchased and downloaded it will be accessible from the iPad app.

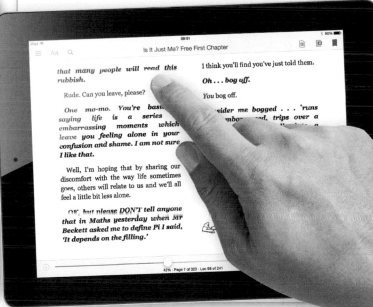

Reading Tips

When you first open an e-book in Kindle, a list of reading tips pops up. These will make reading your e-books much easier so please take notice.

View Settings

With your e-book open, press the Menu button and select View options. Here you can change the font size, background colour (black with white text seems to work well) and screen brightness.

Create a Bookmark

To create a bookmark on any page, press Menu and then Bookmark +. You will see the corner of the page folded over showing the page is marked. You can remove a bookmark in the same way.

Jump to bookmark

The next time you open the e-book after creating a bookmark, Kindle should jump straight to it. If not, press Menu > Go To > My Notes and Marks, and choose the bookmark you want from the list.

How to use the Maps App

With the latest version of the Maps application, Apple has produced a navigation tool to rival the best GPS route planning tools currently on the market.

Finding Places with Maps

Step 1 Start Maps by tapping the app icon on the home screen. To find your current location tap the button with an arrow in it at the bottom left of the screen. To determine the direction you're facing, tap the arrow button at the bottom left a second time.

To search for a specific location, type the address, postcode/zip code or road name into the search field at the top of the screen. If there's more than one match you will be shown a list. Tap on the correct one to find it.

Step 2 To get more information on any location you've selected, tap the blue information button next to the name of the location. From the box that pops up, you can get directions, bookmark the location or assign the location to a contact.

Step 3 To change the view, tap the "i" icon at the bottom right of the screen. You can then select from Standard, Satellite which displays a photographic map or Hybrid which displays the photographic map with street and town names overlaid onto it.

Step 4 You can search for a business by entering the business name or type, for example hairdressers, into the search field at the top of the screen. Pins will then appear on the map indicating all matching businesses in the area.

For directions and contact numbers for each business tap the blue information button next to the appropriate pin. You can zoom in and out at any time by pinching the screen. To move around the maps simply swipe with your finger in any direction.

Using Route Planning

Step 1
To get directions at any time tap the directions button and enter a start point and destination in the Start and End fields that pop-up. You can select the mode of transport (car, public transport or on foot) you plan to use.

Alternatively you can select any location currently pinned, tap the blue information button next to the name and select directions to or direction from. You can also tap the small car icon next to the name to see a route.

Step 2
Maps will quickly calculate the best route, based on the mode of transport you chose, and display it on the map marked as a blue line. The total distance, and estimated travel time will be displayed at the top of the screen.

Step 3
If there are alternative routes available, these will also be displayed as lighter blue lines. You can switch between routes by tapping the label marked Route 2, Route 3, etc. Distance and travel time will update for each route selected.

Step 4
You can view a written step-by-step breakdown of the route by tapping the small 3-line icon that appears beside the 3D button at the bottom-left of the screen. Tap the icon again to close this list of directions.

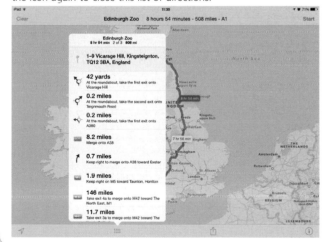

Traffic Information

You can get traffic information at any time by tapping or dragging the curled corner of the map at the bottom right of the screen. Tap Show Traffic and current conditions will be displayed on main roads. Red means the road is very busy and green means traffic is flowing smoothly. You can turn traffic information off at any time by tapping the page button then tapping Hide Traffic.

When traffic information is turned on, you will also see small workman signs at various places. This means that there are scheduled roadworks happening in those locations. Tap any of the workman icons and then tap the information icon to get more details, including possible length of delays and how long the works will continue.

Using turn-by-turn Navigation

Step 1 Find your destination and select a route using the guides shown on the preceding pages (Finding Places with Maps and Route Planning). When you are happy with your chosen route, tap the blue Start button in the top-right corner.

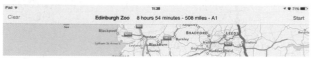

Step 2 The map will automatically zoom in at the start of your route and a large motorway-style sign will appear at the top of the map screen. These show the distance to the next change of direction, warn of roundabouts, etc.

Step 3 As you travel along your route, the instructions will scroll across the top of the screen. As each new instruction scrolls onto screen, spoken instructions will also be played. These can only be turned off using the main volume controls.

Step 4 You can scan through your route by scrolling the instruction signs manually. As you do this, the camera will also scroll along the route to show you the change of direction, roundabout, etc.

Step 5 You can zoom in on the map at any time, even whilst the turn-by-turn directions are being shown. To do this, simply double-tap anywhere along the route line. To zoom back out, you will need to use the pinch-to-zoom method.

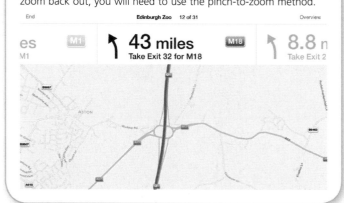

Step 6 You can also view an overview of the route at any time by tapping the Overview button in the top-right corner of the screen. Whilst in overview, you can see a written list of directions by tapping the list icon in the bottom-left corner.

Viewing Locations in 3D

Step 1 Before you can properly view the maps in 3D, you need to switch to either Hybrid or Satellite view. In standard view the maps will still look flat. Tap the "i" icon. and select your view preference.

Step 2 To now switch to 3D view, tap the small 3D button in the bottom-left corner of the map screen. You will notice that the camera angle shifts when you do this. If you are zoomed out, you will hardly notice any difference.

Step 3 Zoom in to the map and you will start to see contours, hills and valleys rendered before your very eyes. The 3D feature can slow things down if you are using a slow Wi-Fi or 3G connection, but not by much.

Step 4 If you are viewing a large city that has rendered 3D buildings, you can increase the camera angle to allow you to see the buildings better. When this is available, you will see the 3D button change to a building button.

3D Buildings

The 3D feature of the new Maps app really comes alive when you are viewing a big city such as London or New York. When you are viewing a city, you can actually see buildings rising out of the map. You can zoom around Big Ben or fly up the side of the Empire State Building. It is probably impossible to extend this amazing feature to every building, but it would be a pretty impressive thing to see!

Complete i

How to use the
Game Center App

Playing on your own is fun but let's be honest – playing with and against friends is even better. With this app you can do this any time you want.

The Game Center App's Key Features Explained

We've highlighted the key features of this application to help you understand better how it works.

This total shows you and other Game Center friends the number of games you have played.

Your total number of Game Center friends is shown here.

These app links are recommended to your tastes, tap once to be taken to the App Store.

This total show the number of Achievements you have completed on your iPad.

Customise your display by clicking any of these five options to focus on that key content.

I like the sound of that. How do I get involved?

As well you should. Open Game Center and set up your account. You'll need to come up with a unique handle for yourself that will be your Game Center ID. You can then add friends to your list using their Game Center handle or email address.

Yes, I've done all that. How do I start playing?

You can search for all kinds of games on the App Store. However Game Center enables you to search specifically for Game Center supported games. You'll be taken to the App Store automatically where you can browse, read reviews and buy titles as normal.

Adding a Photo to Your Profile

To inject a little more of your personality into your Game Center profile you can also upload a photo. For this short guide we will take you through each step of the process.

Step 1   Tap the blank photo icon beside your user-name on the Game Center main screen.

Step 2   Either upload an existing photo or take one with the iPad camera.

Step 3   Take your picture and when you are happy with it, hit the "Use" button.

Step 4   The rest of your friends list - current and future - can now view your new profile image.

NOTE: To change your image simply repeat the process.

It's really that easy!

With Game Center set up you'll be able to add your scores to online leaderboards, challenge friends, make new friends and receive notifications of special events and further developments in the gaming world.

THE ESSENTIAL
iPAD APP
STARTER KIT

Over the years there have been many classic apps available for the iPad, but we aren't going to look back over the App Store archives. Instead we have chosen our picks of the very best apps from the current generation. What you'll find on the following pages are the apps that our team of experts have picked out as the best software you can find for your iPad, covering the very best of the 23 categories that make up the App Store. Every app that is featured here can be considered an essential and will show off the power of your iPad to the fullest.

Flipboard:
Your Social News Magazine

Developer: **Flipboard, Inc**
Price: **£0.79 US$1.25 0,99€**

Wouldn't it be great if you had a magazine that was entirely dedicated to you and the things that you're interested in? That's what Flipboard is, or at least that's what it appears to be thanks to the fantastic interface. It gathers RSS feeds, as well as tweets from your Twitter friends and Facebook updates, and reformats them into magazine-style pages. You turn the pages with a swipe, and a page-turning animation adds to the sensation of reading a glossy magazine. It comes with several general RSS feeds pre-installed, but you can delete these and easily add your own by searching for categories or keywords. The great thing about it is the way it looks and it makes keeping in touch with everything so much more friendly and appealing. Rather than Tweets appearing as links, you'll get images and text from the actual articles themselves, which you can then click on to read the whole thing if you're interested. Everything is pulled into Flipboard and formatted in its own clear style. This really is a superb app and one that everyone should check out.

Stephen Hawking's Snapshots of the Universe

Developer: **Random House Digital, Inc.**
Price: **£2.99 US$4.99 3,99€**

Steven Hawking is considered by many to be the world's greatest - and most famous - scientist of our time! Hawking was Lucasian Professor of Mathematics at the University of Cambridge for 30 years; he is a world-famous astrophysicist, theoretical physicist, cosmologist; and an author of several books, including A Brief History of Time, The Universe in a Nutshell, Black Holes and Baby Universe, amongst others! All in all, a phenomenal man with an equally phenomenal mind. Over the years, Hawking has shared his advanced understanding and knowledge of the universe by offering the world simplified explanations of these concepts so that the likes of myself and many others without PhDs can understand them. Recently, Hawking has teamed up with eBook and app publisher, Random House Digital, and has developed his first official iOS app to help simplify these concepts even more in the form of a fully interactive iPad app specifically designed for both children and adults alike. Steven

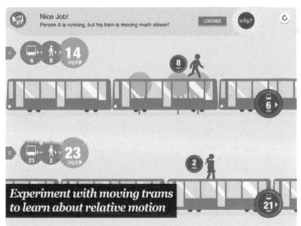

Experiment with moving trams to learn about relative motion

Hawking's Snapshots of the Universe teaches users the principles that control our universe via eight simple, yet entertaining interactive experiments (mini-games). The interactive elements within these experiments allow you to spin planets around and put them into orbit within your own solar system to better understand the theory of relativity, drop objects with Galileo to learn about gravity, discover Einstein's warped worldview and G-force in outer space, search for black holes in the constellation of Leo, and much more! For each of the eight experiments (mini-games), you get a brief overview, the fully interactive experiment itself, and a much more in-depth analysis to go with it. Each experiment is specifically designed for the iPad, so the interactive elements are smooth at all times, allowing you to effortlessly slingshot planets into orbit; tilt your device to alter the gravity; move sliders to adjust relative speed; and much more. Each experiment is explained in layman's terms and is reduced to its simplest form for easy understanding of the concept. Additionally, there are pop-ups that help guide you forwards, and by tapping the "Why?" icon, you can reveal a much more in-depth discussion of said topic! There are even video discussions from Hawking himself, which help to reinforce these concepts. Snapshots of the Universe most certainly is not a substitute for reading A Brief History of Time, however it is definitely enough to inspire young scientists - and even adults - who want to learn more about our universe!

The Poetry App

Developer: Josephine Hart Poetry Foundation
Price: Free

 The Poetry App is a beautifully presented feature-rich application that offers its more sophisticated readers over 115 poems written by 16 of the world's greatest poets of all time! Upon opening the app, the first thing you notice is just how gorgeous the main menu screen is, displaying a feature-rich study with simple navigation options represented by gold-rimmed picture frames. The 'Explore Poems' picture is where the magic happens, giving you access to all the available poems. Now, you can simply read the poems yourself; however Josephine Hart believed "that poetry truly comes alive when read aloud", and that's reflected wonderfully in this app, as each poem is accompanied by high-quality recordings by truly talented voice-actors, including the likes of Dan Stevens, Juliet Stephenson, Dominic West, Charles Dance, Sinead Cusack, Simon Callow and Jeremy Irons! In addition, you can also view a brief description of the 'Narrators'; save your favourite poems to your 'Favourites' list; read up on 'Josephine Hart' herself, who also puts each poem into context to help you better understand their meaning; and you can even write and record your own poems from within the app, saving them into the 'My Poems' section! A truly magnificent app for poetry enthusiasts.

Castle of Illusion
Starring Mickey Mouse

Perfect for Grandkids

Developer: Disney | Price: £6.99 US$9.99 7,99€

Castle of Illusion Starring Mickey Mouse is a remastered version of the classic 16-bit Sega Genesis/Mega Drive retro platformer from 1990, and what a fantastic game it still is to this day! The game itself is exactly like the original (although slightly re-imagined), and now with much more appealing visuals and smoother controls. Thankfully the game stays true to itself with the majority of gameplay taking place in vivid 2D settings, with the option to enter a 3D perspective seamlessly for added exploration, which is nice! The controls are responsive and work well with Mickey's limited abilities: there are two different control options to choose, a virtual button control i.e. left/right buttons on the left, and a jump button on the right. Or by default you can move Mickey using the left side of the screen and flick up on the right side to jump. Both control settings have an awkwardly placed action button too, which allows Mickey to launch projectiles (apples) at enemies, and/or open chests for treasure. Additionally, the game also supports a compatible controller if this is more your strong suit! Sadly, for a premium-priced game, Castle of Illusion is incredibly short, offering players a total game-time of roughly 6 hours! That said, there are many challenges to complete and collectables/achievements to acquire; therefore replayability is worth it!

Biography –
A Journey With History's Most Influential People

Developer: MAMN84 | Price: £2.99 $4.99 3,99€

The world that we live in today has been created by hundreds of influential people over the centuries; and their talents, inventions, and discoveries have cleverly crafted what we currently know today. This interactive history book is an extensive biography of the world's most renowned philosophers, scientists, physicians, political leaders, artists and composers, such as the likes of: Abraham Lincoln, Albert Einstein, Archimedes, Beethoven, Benjamin Franklin, Christopher Columbus, Da Vinci, Galileo, Gandhi, Genghis Khan, George Washington, Isaac Newton, John F Kennedy, Martin Luther King, Jr, Mozart, Picasso, Queen Victoria, Shakespeare, Sigmund Freud, Stephen Hawking, Winston Churchill, Van Gogh, and many, many more!! This app is designed specifically for iPads, and contains an in-depth biography of all 100 influential people; including high quality photos, audio accompaniment, and stunning illustrations. You will have access to a full description of their lives, accomplishments, major events, quotes, contributions, and death if applicable. Visually, this app looks incredible; the presentation is stunning; and the information is extensive. This truly is a wonderful app, and by far the best of its kind! So if you're interested in learning about the most significant people in the history of the world, then download this app now and prepare to be amazed.

BADLAND

Developer: **Simogo** | Price: **£2.49 US$3.99 2,99€**

BADLAND is a beautifully designed side-scrolling action adventure puzzle platformer that takes place in an atmospheric forest, packed full of deadly traps that you must navigate through to reach the end of each level. The game is controlled by using one finger to guide the peculiar furry character through the treacherous BADLAND, much like the highly addictive 2D Helicopter PC game if you recall; or the side scrolling sections in classic Mario, however, this is a great deal more in-depth and obviously visually superior. The screen automatically scrolls from left to right and you must simply tap your iDevice screen in order to cause the fur-ball to rise higher, thus avoiding the many traps and obstacles in your path. Releasing your finger causes him to drop back down. There are many power-ups available in each level, which you will need to collect (or avoid, depending on what traps are coming up) in order to complete each stage.

For example some will make you larger or smaller, thus causing you to become heavier or lighter, affecting whether you can squeeze through small spaces; some will transform you into a ball, allowing you to roll across treacherous grounds; and others will turn you invisible. There are numerous contraptions you will need to use (or avoid) too; for example circular saws, which will inevitably kill you; or catapults, which will propel you up to otherwise unreachable areas. Selecting the incorrect power or contraption could make it impossible to complete the level, so your decision is vital. There are 40 unique levels to complete, and each one offers a totally different experience. There are so many challenges in each level that it will undoubtedly take you several attempts to figure out exactly what to do. This is where trial and error and the addictiveness seriously take control. The gameplay is excellent, so you'd imagine the visuals would let it down in some way. But this is definitely not the case! The art style is actually what grabs you the most, using vivid colours for each level background and dark silhouettes for the characters and foreground. This truly is a fantastic game. There is also a local online multiplayer feature which allows up to four players to battle it out on the same iDevice over 16 levels. This feature is all about survival - steal power-ups, hinder opponents, and survive to the end.

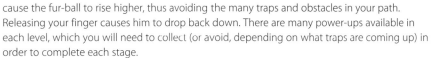

Perfect for Gamers

Real Racing 3

Developer: **Electronic Arts** Price: **Free**

We've previously reviewed more arcade-like rally racing games, but now it's time to move on to the more realistic road-racing experience; and we guarantee that you won't find anything else on iOS better than this! Real Racing 3 is currently the No.1 top free app in 90 countries worldwide and here's why. For starters, it looks more like a PS3 or XBox 360 game than anything else! Using an advanced Mint 3 Engine, the game features realistic weather conditions, light glare and dynamic reflections, impressive vehicle damage, and even fully functional rear view mirrors. The game's extensive vehicle list includes more than 50 cars in total from leading manufacturers, including Porsche, Lamborghini, Dodge, Bugatti, and many more. Each vehicle can be upgraded with parts to maximise overall performance. Real Racing 3 also uses real tracks and real locations, including Mazda Raceway, Laguna Seca and Silverstone to name a few! EA have also focused more on the Online Multiplayer side of things by using an innovative new Time Shifted Multiplayer feature. But the most impressive part of all is the game's longevity, which allows you to compete in over 1,000 events including Cup Races, Eliminations, Endurance Challenges, and Drag Races. This really is next gen' racing!

forScore

Developer: **forScore, LLC** | Price: **£4.99 US$6.99 5,49€**

 ForScore was the very first app of its kind and over the years and many updates, it's now by far the best sheet music viewer available for the iPad! ForScore is entirely PDF-based and is capable of reading any PDF file, which is most definitely its strongest selling point. Initially you will have to save all of your music scores in PDF format and then load them into forScore via iTunes file sharing (which is by far the easiest way to do so); Email or DropBox, which is useful when on the move; and other file-sharing apps such as GoodReader for instance! Additionally, the app has the ability to use its own built-in web browser to save PDF files of sheet music direct from the web into the app. Once you've loaded your score sheets, you can then save and organise them for easy access however you see fit i.e. Title, Composer, Genre, Keywords and more. ForScore uses PDF metadata to circulate the various 'Search and Find' options; for instance, you can organise your music into Set Lists and display them in several ways i.e. the order in which you entered them; alphabetically; recently played; or shuffle/random. When reading a score sheet, turning the pages is quick and easy – either tap the far right side of the screen, or swipe left to right (which we found to be the easier option). Tapping the screen reveals the menu options, and tapping the Title reveals a dialog box displaying metadata. All the familiar iPad pinch and zoom gestures work here too. Bookmarks can be added to any page you like and searching for said bookmarks is effortless. One of our favourite features is the ability to attach an audio file (song) to a music sheet so that you can read the score sheet as the song is playing! There is a standard metronome that can be used; however ⋯ you can also attach a unique BPM number to each score sheet and then set the pages to turn automatically based on the tempo and beats/measure per score, which is incredibly useful as it eliminates the need to manually turn each page! You can also move, copy/paste, and delete pages from any score; as well as being able to add files direct from DropBox. There are some minor features also that help enhance the experience even

more i.e. a pitch source; an on-screen piano keyboard; and support for AirPlay so that you can view your score sheets on the big screen. Additionally you can annotate your sheets however you desire with annotation tools such as draw, erase, and clear. There are various drawing styles at hand too, including hue, saturation, transparency, brightness and size. Finally, you can have different versions of the same sheet (24 in total) and each one varies in metadata and annotations. If there are any files that you want to share with other musicians, that can be done effortlessly via AirDrop, Messages, Emails and more!

Disney Storytime

Developer: **Disney** | Price: **£FREE**

With the initial free download, you get access to three digital Disney storybooks including "Monsters Inc: Always Time For A Laugh", "Tangled: Rapunzel's Story" and "Toy Story 3: Starry Night". There are 18 other Disney books available for download via a child-friendly credit system, which can be bought via in-app purchases. Parents pre-purchase these credits via IAP, which children can then use at any time to unlock whichever books they want! One credit unlocks one book. '2 Story Credits' cost £2.49; '10 Story Credits' costs £6.99; and '21 Story Credits' for £12.99 allows you to unlock all available Disney books in the app, including "The Little Mermaid", "Aladdin", "Cars", "Finding Nemo", "Incredibles", "Cinderella", "Sleeping Beauty", "Wall-E", "Lion King", and more! Each storybook features wonderful illustrations, gorgeous animations, original music, and hundreds of appropriate sound effects. Clear and professional voice narration is also available, which highlights the written word as it is spoken to help improve reading skills. Additional reading options allow you to read through the story yourself, and record your own voice to narrate over the top. Download the "Philip's Disney Storylight" as a companion app via the App Store and use it with Disney Storytime, which will emit beautiful coloured lighting effects around the room synchronised in time with the story - very clever!

Perfect for Babysitting

WaterIn

Developer: **Mothership Software Ltd**
Price: **Free**

Staying hydrated is important but it's something that's easily overlooked in day-to-day life. This very simple but effective app is designed to ensure you always remember to drink your recommended two litres per day. It does this with a very simple on-screen display which is basically a sequence of eight blue bars in a colour gradient. Each bar represents one 25cl glass of water. Each time you take a drink you have to

tap the Drink button and select the approximate size of the drink you had. The bars will drain away by the appropriate amount so you can see exactly how close you are to drinking your day's quota. You can set it up to send you push notifications to remind you to take a drink, and that's pretty much all there is to it. If you're worried you're not getting enough water down you on a daily basis then this is an app you should consider trying.

Cool Escapes

Developer: **teNeues Digital Media GmbH** | Price: **£3.99 US$5.99 4,99€**

Getting away from the daily stresses of work, bills and screaming children is necessary at certain times; however, do you really want to go on holiday to relax and still be surrounded by the usual hustle and bustle of other families and kids?

Probably not! Well that's where Cool Escapes come in, as it provides you with over 100 specially selected luxury resorts for the ultimate R & R holiday. These magical resorts are absolute paradise, from the natural jungles of Costa Rica to the quiet hillside towns of Italy. These resorts have been selected for people who truly want to get away from their hectic lifestyle to completely immerse themselves in their relaxation period. The app allows you to search for resorts by world areas and country, and contains a full description of each hotel; as well as interesting facts about the location, full

addresses and phone numbers, a direct web link, and of course an extensive photo gallery of stunning high-resolution pictures of each resort. So, if you fancy the ultimate break with just that little bit more magic than a regular holiday, then this app is definitely for you. New luxury resorts and locations are updated regularly, so keep a look out for the perfect romantic getaway!

Temppo ·
Minimalist Weather

Developer: **Joao Pescada** | Price: **£0.69 US$0.99 0,79€**

Temppo · Minimalist Weather is exactly what the title suggests: "minimalist". If you're looking for a feature-rich weather app with maps, radars, graphs, and advanced weather-related data, then this app is not for you. If however you're simply looking for a clean and elegant weather app that displays the current weather conditions and the temperature for an instant forecast update at a glance, then this is the app for you! Everything about this app is visual-based - for instance, the colour of the screen changes

depending on the current temperature of your current location i.e. red/orange represents a higher temperature, whereas green/blue indicates a lower temperature! Secondly, the weather-based animations (sun, cloud, rain etc.) are large, clear, and placed directly in the centre of the screen, perfect for a quick glance. The temperature is also large and clearly visible at the bottom of the screen. Finally, you'll be given the current weather condition in words also, accompanied by a brief thought/feeling, which is nice i.e. "Overcast: at least it's not raining yet", for instance. Additional features allow you to check the forecast for 'Later That Day' and for 'Tomorrow' by swiping vertically on screen, access the 'Options Menu' by swiping horizontally on screen, and you can also switch between Fahrenheit and Celsius depending on your location.

Sherlock: The Network HD

Developer: **Simogo** | Price: **£2.49 US$3.99 2,99€**

Loyal fans of BBC1's hit TV drama, Sherlock, will be pleased to know that the long-awaited iPhone app, Sherlock: The Network, has finally arrived, giving fans an exciting new adventure in iOS game form! You take on the role of an unnamed member of Sherlock's homeless network at which you must assist Sherlock (Benedict Cumbernatch), John (Martin Freeman) and Mycroft (Mark Gatiss) on ten new and exclusive cases, as you virtually navigate your way around London on foot, by tube, or by taxi; speaking to witnesses, gathering evidence, searching for clues, collecting money, and solving puzzles and challenges to in turn solve the mysteries at hand! Throughout your adventure, Sherlock, John and Mycroft address you directly via new and exclusive video footage shot on the sets of series three! Travelling around via tube (which is the fastest and most cost-effective means of transport) presents you with the first of many challenging mini games that make up the game, i.e. the tube mini game for instance requires you to piece together different

coloured sections of the track around a grid to enable the train to successfully travel from one location to another. This may sound easy enough; however, the challenge is made more difficult due to the fact that the pieces that you're provided with initially may be incorrect, and the train may begin to travel along the incomplete track before the correct pieces become available – therefore speed is crucial in your success! Speed also means points, i.e. the faster you complete a challenge, the more points you will earn; and bearing in mind there is a Global Leaderboard, replayability is fantastic too, as you will undoubtedly find yourself replaying challenges in order to beat your previous time and ultimately rank higher on the Leaderboard! Other challenges and puzzles require you to unscramble audio tracks, crack codes, break into password-protected email accounts, and overcome visual observation challenges in search of vital clues regarding the current case! Additionally, you even get to snoop around Sherlock's Baker Street room, which is a nice touch. Again, all challenges are timed and your final time upon completion is added to the Global Leaderboard. The challenges puzzles start off relatively easy, but get progressively more difficult as you advance through the game. Finally, it's off to your Mind Palace where you must piece together all the clues that you've uncovered prior to this, and solve the case by sifting through the clues from an assortment of whirling words and phrases! Once you successfully solve one case, you move swiftly onto the next. Sherlock: the Network is challenging, addictive, entertaining, and offers its users a replayablity factor second to none – all in all, a fantastic mystery game!

Use Your Handwriting

Developer: **Gee Whiz Stuff** | Price: **Free**

Many people who have switched from button phones to touchscreen Apple devices find that typing on the pop-up keyboard is one of the biggest problems. Sometimes when I'm in a rush, it looks as if a chimpanzee has written it! If that sounds familiar, then the Use Your Handwriting app for iPhones and iPads will appeal to you greatly, as it allows you to use your finger as a pen instead of the pop-up keyboard to write quick notes, reminders, lists, and even messages and emails to other people. The app uses an advanced Handwriting Engine like no other, which significantly increases the accuracy of picking up each individual's handwriting, and is ideal for quickly jotting down something in a hurry, such as a shopping list. There's a useful tutorial users-guide that explains all the basic functions, and you can select either right or left handed. You can choose between five unique writing styles, from professional Sharp to wonderful Calligraphy, as well as being able to change the colour and thickness of your handwriting too. You can then share your artistic writing via email, Facebook and Twitter. This is a fantastic replacement for pen and paper, and if you like this free app, then you can upgrade to GOLD for even more features.

Pinterest

Developer: **Pinterest Inc**
Price: **Free**

When you break it down Pinterest is basically a photo sharing app that enables you to find, like and share images with friends from around the web. It's set up with a slightly different emphasis though. The idea is that it builds up to become your own personal wall of inspiration for whatever you may be doing, planning or dreaming of doing in your life. From great holiday destinations that you stumble across to cool knick-knacks or present ideas, Pinterest is a place to store them so you can refer back to them whenever you want. Most of us surf the web probably every day and you're sure to have come across countless cool things that you've completely forgotten about five minutes later. Pinterest enables you to 'pin' them to a virtual noticeboard which will eventually become packed with all the things you love. What's not to dig about that?

TuneIn Radio

Developer: **Synsion Radio Technologies** | Price: **Free**

Ever get bored of your iTunes playlist or just want something different to listen to once in a while? Installing TuneIn Radio will open up a vast new range of possibilities, giving you access to more than 40,000 local radio stations around the world broadcasting on the AM and FM wavelengths.

It's not just a tuner though. You get a comprehensive listing split into categories including music, sports, news and talk. This enables you to search specific shows to find one that appeals to you personally and go straight to it rather than spending ages bouncing from channel to channel. When you find a show or channel you like you don't have to miss anything as you can pause and rewind up to 30 minutes at any time just like you can on live TV with things like Sky Plus. Furthermore you can record any station you find using a built in timer. This is great if there's s specific show you're interested in but aren't able to listen at the time of broadcast. Podcasts are also available to listen to and there's the facility to bookmark categories, stations and even specific shows that you like.

This is a virtually faultless piece of software for anyone anywhere who enjoys listening to radio, music or anything else. The option to view schedules is superb, the search functions are exhaustive and the level of functionality is simply remarkable, yet it's so easy to use. Just load it up and you're away. A whole world of audio entertainment awaits you. The only drawback that we can come up with is, as with any streaming software, if you're on a data allowance it will quickly get used up so always try to connect to a Wi-Fi network if possible. That's no fault of the app though, which is just completely brilliant.

Skype

Developer: **Skype Software** | Price: **Free**

Skype is the perfect way to communicate with friends, relatives and business contacts face to face, no matter where you or they may be. The official Skype iPad app turns your iPad into a full-screen video messaging device. If you already have a Skype account all you need to do is log in and all your contacts will automatically be transferred to your iPad. It works via Wi-Fi or 3G, enabling you to chat completely free of charge with anyone else who has the Skype app or

client installed. Further subscription-based services are also available that enable you to make calls to landlines and mobile phones and even receive calls on your iPad. If you want to take advantage of these features they're there, but the basic functions alone make Skype an absolute must-have for everyone. If you haven't used it before you don't know what you're missing. Whether you're talking to relatives who've moved away or conducting long-distance business meetings, the scope and potential make this an invaluable tool for everyone.

Wikipanion for iPad

Developer: **Robert Chin** | Price: **FREE**

With this app, accessing Wikipedia has never been faster or easier. It has been designed to allow users to easily search, navigate and display all Wikipedia entries. It streamlines your browsing with history grouped by visit date, and bookmarks that not only link individual entries, but individual sections within an entry. Essentially Wikipanion is really just the Wikipedia website optimised for iPad and packaged with a couple of usability enhancements built in, but it does make researching subjects on Wikipedia much quicker and easier to organise. Apart from giving you access to the full range of publicly maintained knowledge within Wikipedia, Wikipanion gives you a separate table of contents for each article and the accompanying categories that match it. The inclusion of quick sharing links via Facebook and Twitter rounds off what is simply the best way to view Wikipedia from your iPad.

eBay for iPad

Developer: **eBay Inc.** | Price: **FREE**

There are many applications available from the App Store that enable you to access core elements or enhance features of your eBay account, yet unlike its competitors for your iPad this app is fully endorsed and produced by eBay themselves. It allows registered eBay users quick, easy and most importantly familiar access to all of the key information from their eBay account. As the application has developed from its frankly limited original guise to the current version where there are no limitations on your activity, this really does live up to its moniker, that being eBay on the go. Basically if you are an active user of eBay, this is simply a must have app for your iPad. Offering not simply a simplified mobile version masquerading as an application, eBay mobile's title is also the perfect summation of the functionality of this app. This offers an enhanced version of the web alternative, which will quickly become your, as it is our, first destination when it comes to listing, viewing or shopping on eBay. eBay Mobile.

BeFunky Photo Editor for iPad

Developer: **BeFunky**
Price: **FREE**

You can turn even the most mundane and boring photos into stylised works of art with this terrific app from BeFunky. It's a highly flexible photo editor that couldn't be simpler for even the most clueless novices to use. You start off by choosing an image from your image library, or you can take a picture right from the app. When you've chosen a snap the main controls appear at the top of the screen. First you can set the brightness, contrast, hue and saturation via series of sliders. You can also sharpen the image, rotate and crop it. Once you're happy you can choose from a long list of filters to add lots of cool effects. Finally you get to choose a frame before saving the image and there's the option to share it direct to Facebook and Flickr. The filters in conjunction with the various adjustment sliders give you a great deal of control to really add interest to your boring old snaps. A great app.

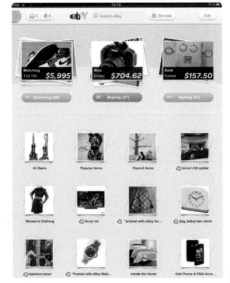

Worms Crazy Golf HD

Developer: **Team17 Software Lmt** | Price: **£0.69 US$0.99 0,79€**

The peculiar Worms franchise has been around for almost 20 years now. And for the first time in Worms history, the developers have managed to cater not just for their existing fans, but for everyone else by incorporating something that we all know and love: Crazy Golf. Not just that, but this instalment is actually much easier to get the hang of, unlike previous titles, which were a nightmare to master. Crazy Golf HD has you controlling a single Worm for starters, instead of the usual army of Worms. Secondly, your goal isn't to destroy the opposing Worms, but instead to hit the ball into the hole in as few shots as possible. Sliding your finger across the screen will rotate the camera angle around for a better view of the course. You can then move a small aiming reticule to line up your shot; and then press and hold the Hit button to increase power, and release the button to take the shot. Simple! The challenge comes however when trying to avoid the many hazards each insane course has to offer i.e. exploding sheep, suicidal worms, ball-stealing moles, teleport pads, cannons, magnets, and more! There are three 18-hole courses to play through, and many unique challenges; as well as a variety of unlockables and achievements, and the ability to upgrade your Clubs. All-in-all, crazy fun!

Home and Dry

Developer: **MetDesk** | Price: **£1.49 US$1.99 1,59€**

Home and Dry by MetDesk was designed specifically to help people living in the UK and Ireland keep track of approaching storms and heavy rainfall. The "5 minute, 1km Rain Radar" specific to UK/Ireland is the highest-quality Rain Radar available! The information is animated at 5-minute intervals for the previous two hours, overlaid on a fully-interactive map at which you can get accurate rain forecast details up to two hours ahead. The app uses your GPS location to pinpoint your current position and in turn provides you with current localised weather information. You can also add location markers for points of interest and instantly get rainfall info for these locations. Switch between Observed Radar and Forecast Rader to get a clear understanding of where the rain is hitting, how heavy it is and what direction it's shifting to in regards to your current position; and with the five-minute intervals, you can see exactly what time it will rain and for how long! You also have access to animated forecast maps for UK and Europe - these are not as sophisticated, but they are incredibly accurate, and additionally provide you with a 7-day forecast clearly displaying Rainfall, Temperature, Cloud Cover, Wind, Jet Stream and Weather Symbols. Sharing options are available too.

Barcode
Scanner HD

Developer: **Vision Smarts** | Price: **£0.69 US$0.99 0,79€**

 There are several Barcode Scanning apps available for iPhones, iPads and iPod Touch, and they all do pretty much the same thing. So what makes Barcode Scanner HD better than all the rest? Well, the premise is the same as any other - point your iDevice camera at any barcode on any item by lining up the red line, and wait for it to turn green. Simple. You will then be shown thousands of online stores that sell the same product in order to find out which store sells it for the cheapest price! You have immediate access to all major retailers such as Amazon UK, Play.com, Tesco, Langton Info, One Click Pharmacy, Alibris, Zavvi, Boots.com, John Lewis, Debenhams, Pixmania, and many more. But what makes Barcode Scanner HD stand out above all the rest is its scanning speed (which is faster than its competitors), accuracy (which successfully scans barcodes even if they are damaged or blurred), customers' reviews assigned to each product, and the ability to scan QR Codes also, which others fail to do. You can also add products to your Wishlist at Wishlist.com, as well as multiple sharing options i.e. Facebook and Twitter. So, if you're a savvy shopper and want your items at the cheapest price possible, then look no further.

Secret Apps

Developer: **Sensible Code** | Price: **£0.69 US$0.99 0,79€**

 Nowadays, we leave our iPhone or iPad on the side for 30 seconds, and all of a sudden we have family members, friends, and young children rummaging through it looking for pictures, videos, music, and games, which has unfortunately made security and protection of private data massively important! Well not to worry, as Secret Apps has you covered. Secret Apps is essentially a 'wall safe' for absolutely anything in your iDevice that you don't want other people to see - private pictures, videos, bookmarks, web browsing history, contacts, notes, documents, files, and so on. Store whatever you want within the app, and the app cleverly disguises itself as a regular app folder on your home screen. There is also a Decoy Mode, which distracts unwanted visitors from locating your actual access point. The folder is password protected with either a 4-digit PIN code, or a

personal Pattern-lock, depending on your preference. If anyone attempts to open the folder or tries to crack the code, the front-facing camera will snap a picture of them trying to do so, so that you can catch them in the act! The app will then alert you with an icon badge, log the incident in a secure file within the app, and store the picture of the intruder for when you next return to your device. There is a Photo Vault feature within the app itself, which allows you to store all your private photos and videos within it, and the app itself contains a fast and intuitive photo viewer, which allows you to create multiple albums, and view all your photos and videos via a slideshow without the need to

cancel out of Secret Apps and thus lose protection. You can also take private photos and videos from within the app itself. The same applies for the Private Web Browser feature, which enables you to browse the web from within the app (much like Mobile Safari) so that all your web browsing remains secret. Secret Apps web browser supports multiple tabs, downloading of videos, and by holding your finger over any image, you can automatically save it to your Photo Vault. This is a fantastic app for anyone who has private data on their iOS, and wants to add another layer of security to their device. Not even Houdini could crack this one - definitely worth it!

Backflip Madness

Developer: **Gamesoul Studio**
Price: **£0.69 US$0.99 0,79€**

Backflip Madness is a fast-paced, free-running game that requires precise timing when jumping to avoid the many obstacles in your path. Graphically, Backflip Madness is terrible, using basic 2D and 3D graphics for its level backgrounds and chav-like runner. However, this is one of the most addictive games we've ever played and it will either have you hooked instantly or make you want to throw your iDevice at the wall! Probably both. The game is controlled using a single button. As you run through each level, simply tap the button to begin crouching. When you reach a deadly drop, press it again to jump. While airborne, tap it again to tuck in your legs and perform tricks. And then tap it a final time to land on the other side. How can something so simple become so frustratingly addictive? Well there are three difficulty settings to master, and if you fail a level on the final jump, you'll undoubtedly HAVE TO try again, there are also new locations and back flips to unlock; difficult achievements and challenges to complete; and an overall leader board that you'll want to be top of! If you can ignore its hideous appearance and accept it for what it is, then you'll love it. But prepare to be annoyed!

DEVICE 6

Developer: **Simogo** | Price: **£2.49 US$3.99 2,99€**

DEVICE 6 is the latest instalment from Simogo - the creative minds behind Year Walk, Beat Sneak Bandit, Bumpy Road and Kosmo Spin - and is unlike any other game that we've ever played before! Some people may argue that DEVICE 6 isn't even a game - it can be classed as a gamebook, an interactive novella, an interactive storybook, or all the above. But I believe it's more of a challenging text-based adventure puzzle game! The interactive story is the most important part, and centres around a girl named Anna who wakes up on a remote island in possession of a peculiar-looking doll, with no memory of how she got there. It's your job to find out where she is, how she got there, and most importantly why she is there by solving some of the most challenging puzzles we've ever come across in an iOS game! Much like Year Walk, players are thrown into this interactive world without much direction, only the words on screen to guide you. As you read through the narrative, the words will stretch out, bend, and twist in different directions on screen, requiring you to rotate your iOS device regularly in order to follow the Narrative Map. As you read, you will hear appropriate sounds and sound effects to go with the written word. If the words on screen bend to the right (rotate your device 90 degrees) and Anna will in turn move to the right, at which point you'll find yourself in a new room or new hallway via a new text-screen. DEVICE 6 relies on audio clip recordings and three-dimensional photographs as well as text that you must study repeatedly in order to uncover vital clues. You're therefore advised to play DEVICE 6 with a pen and paper at hand to jot down notes and clues for future reference, as there will be a great deal of backtracking. There are no Lives, Health, Checkpoints, or other features usually found in games; however, if you're unable to complete a particular puzzle, then your punishment is simply that you cannot advance with the story! There are no optional hints to aid you in any way either; therefore if you're stuck, then you're stuck for good until you figure it out! DEVICE 6 sadly won't appeal to everyone; but for those of you who are interested, you really do need to try it out for yourself, as words simply cannot do it justice!

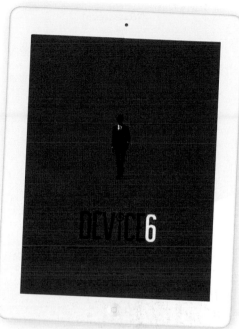

Radio?

Hoping to find

Recommended iPad Accessories

With the release of the iPad mini with Retina display and the iPad Air, Apple's tablet has been elevated beyond all previous recognition, so why not take your essential tablet to a whole new level with our pick of the best accessories you can buy for your iPad.

iPad Smart Case

From: Apple

To help keep your iPad in perfect condition, it is best to get yourself a quality micro fibre case. So while you are at it, why not get one that doubles as a stand so you can watch those videos without having to hold the iPad or balance it precariously? There are numerous cases available but our suggestion would always be this official case available direct from Apple.

iPad mini Smart Cover

From: Apple

Redesigned for iPad mini, the iPad mini Smart Cover is designed to be its perfect match: a thin, durable cover that magnetically aligns for a perfect fit. It automatically wakes and sleeps your iPad mini. It's a handy stand for reading, watching and typing. Its microfibre lining keeps your iPad mini screen clean. And it's a way to make your iPad mini as personal on the outside as it is on the inside.

Disney Creativity Studio Smart Stylus

From: Disney Creativity Studio Smart Stylus

This provides an immersive creative experience with the Disney characters your grandkids know and love. Real Disney artists teach you how to draw your favourite Disney characters, guiding you through intuitive step-by-step tutorials. The Smart Stylus gives an experience amazingly rich and lifelike. Enjoy hours of fun!

Bowers & Wilkins P3 On-Ear Headphones

From: Bowers & Wilkins

P3 headphones reveal whatever you listen to in detail with pristine highs and lows, an open midrange and all round balanced and natural performance. P3 headphones are light and comfortable. With an in-line remote control and mic, you can get the most out of your iPhone, iPod or iPad. Control your iPad without taking it out of your pocket or bag.

JAMBOX

From: Jawbone Wireless Speaker

This is genuinely a piece of hardware which looks as great as it sounds. With it you can share music, movies, games, phone calls and more wirelessly from your iPad, iPhone, iPod touch or any other Bluetooth device—all in pristine stereo sound that fits in the palm of your hand.

HP Photosmart 5520 e-All-in-One Wireless Printer

From: HP

Print and share wirelessly via AirPrint. HP's Photosmart 5520 e-All-in-One Wireless Printer makes printing and sharing wirelessly with your iPhone or iPad easier than ever. Print wirelessly with AirPrint and send scans to email using the vibrant touchscreen.

Belkin In-Car Charger with Lightning
From: Belkin

Charge your iPad on the road with the Belkin Car Charger. The low-profile design means the charger fits neatly on your dashboard, and the rubber grips let you easily insert and remove it from the power outlet. Follow your route or listen to music on the go without worrying about losing charge.

Bose Soundlink Mini
From: Bose

Enjoy your music on the go, everywhere you go. The SoundLink Mini Bluetooth speaker delivers full, natural sound from an ultra-compact speaker that fits in the palm of your hand. It connects wirelessly to your smartphone, tablet or other

Bluetooth device, so you can listen to your music, videos or games anytime, anywhere. Just grab it and go.

Wacom Bamboo Stylus Duo
From: Wacom

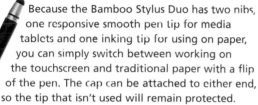

Because the Bamboo Stylus Duo has two nibs, one responsive smooth pen tip for media tablets and one inking tip for using on paper, you can simply switch between working on the touchscreen and traditional paper with a flip of the pen. The cap can be attached to either end, so the tip that isn't used will remain protected.

Bamboo Stylus Duo ensures the most natural pen experience, regardless what media you are using.

Eco + kit screen cleaner
From: Eco

Your iPad screen is prone to dirt, dust and in the case of the touch-screen the dreaded finger grease. Don't be tempted to use standard household cleaning products on the delicate screen,

because they could cause expensive and hard-to-repair damage. Instead you should always use a specialist alcohol and acid free cleaning spray and fibre cloth such as this ECO + kit.

Incase Neoprene Pro Sleeve for iPad mini
From: Incase

The Neoprene Pro Sleeve is Incase's iconic protective solution for iPad. Providing form-fitting, lightweight protection in a simple design, the Neoprene Pro Sleeve works well as a standalone case or inside your favourite bag. Offers complete iPad protection with its form-fitting neoprene construction and plush faux-fur lining.

Belkin's iPad Clearscreen Overlay
From: Belkin

The Belkin Clearscreen Overlay keeps your device looking brand

new, protecting it from scratches and smudges. Its transparency keeps your device looking its stylish self, whilst the application of the overlay is very straightforward; this screen protector won't affect the response of your iPad's touchscreen, it will simply protect it.

Belkin Messenger Bag
From: Belkin

Your iPad offers the freedom to take your home office or your media centre with you wherever you go, but you will want to ensure that the hustle and bustle of travelling doesn't take a toll of your device. When you travel with your iPad, keep it safe from harm with this excellent value over-the-shoulder Belkin Messenger Bag.

AppleCare Protection Plan for iPad
From: Apple

For up to two years from the original purchase date of your iPad, the AppleCare Protection Plan gives you direct, one-stop access to Apple's award-winning telephone technical support for questions about using your iPad. You also get additional service and repair options on your iPad, its battery, and included accessories. An essential!

Glossary of iPad Terms

For those of us who have been using the iPad for a long time and understand all the new words and technical jargon that come with it, it can sometimes be easy to forget that not everyone will understand what we're talking about. We've tried to keep this guide as jargon-free as possible, but inevitably there are some words and phrases that might still seem mysterious to the newcomer. If you're puzzled by anything you've read, we trust you'll find this glossary helpful. If you don't know your iCloud from your iOS, read on...

0-9

3G: The third generation of mobile data networking used by both the iPhone and iPad, this connection is slower than Wi-Fi, but is more readily available and is used to transfer data from your iPad when you are on the go. It uses the mobile phone network.

4G: The fourth generation of mobile data networking offers increased speed when transferring data on the go, but it is still in its early stages of adoption by mobile phone networks.

A

Airplane Mode: All airlines warn you to turn off mobile electronic devices when on board an aircraft, so this iPad setting turns off all incoming and outgoing signals to your device, including data, Bluetooth, and Wi-Fi.

AirPrint: This is a feature of iOS 7 and can be used to print from any iOS device that has been linked to an AirPrint-compatible printer over your home Wi-Fi network.

App: Short for "application", another name for a computer program. An app is a program that has been downloaded on to your iPad from the Apple App Store.

App Store: The App Store is where you can download free and paid programs to your device using your Apple ID. You can access it through the application found on your iPad's home screen.

Apple ID: This is the email address and password that you have registered with Apple. It will be required to access most online applications on your iPad, including iTunes, App Store and iBooks.

B

Bluetooth: Bluetooth is a wireless technology used to link and exchange data with another compatible device. It has a range of approximately 8 metres (25ft). The iPad supports many Bluetooth devices, including headphones, keyboards and hands-free kits.

C

Calendar: This is one of Apple's preloaded apps. Use it to keep track of events, invitations, and reminders on iPhone, iPod touch, and iPad.

Camera: This built-in Apple app is used when taking photos and videos on iPhone and iPod touch 4.

D

Dock: A special row of icons (or Folders post-iOS 4) along the bottom of iPhone, iPod touch and iPad screens, which do not change when you swipe between Home Screens.

F

Facebook: Currently the most popular social networking site on the Internet, Facebook currently has over 835 million registered users.

FaceTime: Apple's video calling service. Requires a Wi-Fi connection and is currently only supported via a phone number on iPhone and Apple ID email address on iPod touch 4 and Mac.

Force Quit: In the Fast App Switcher, tapping and holding an app will put it in Jiggly Mode and tapping the X badge will force it to quit. Built-in apps like Mail and Messages will automatically restart while third-party apps will restart the next time you launch them.

Folder: An icon representing a container for a group of apps. Introduced in iOS 4 they are created by dragging an app on top of the other in Jiggly Mode, and deleted by removing all the apps. iPhone and iPod touch can currently hold 12 apps per Folder. iPad can hold 20.

G

Game Center: Apple's gaming service, where you can discover new games and share your game experiences with friends from around the world.

H

Home Button: The physical hardware button on the front of the iPhone, iPod touch, and iPad, located just below the screen. It's used to wake the device, return to the Home Screen, cycle between the Home Screen and Spotlight Search screen, open the Fast App Switcher, and optionally enable Accessibility features.

Home Screen: The front end of Apple's Springboard app launcher that consists of eleven screens that hold app icons, Folders, the Dock, the Fast App Switcher, and the Spotlight Search screen.

I

iBooks: Apple's eBook reader, available from the App Store. It handles the standard electronic publishing formats protected by FairPlay DRM, and PDF. It was introduced in 2010 along with the iPad.

iCloud: The collective name for Apple's online services, it replaced MobileMe and integrates with all iOS devices and OS X Mac computers.

iOS: Apple mobile operating system and the software that powers the iPhone, iPod touch, iPad, and Apple TV.

iTunes: Mac and Windows music playing software, also used to activate and sync iPhone, iPod touch, and iPad. It is also used to purchase and manage music, movies, TV shows, apps, books, and other media.

iTunes app: iPhone, iPod touch, and iPad app used to access the iTunes Store.

M

Mail: Built-in Apple app for handling POP3, IMAP, MobileMe, and Exchange/ActiveSync email accounts.

Messages: One of Apple's built-in iPhone apps that handles SMS text messages and MMS multimedia messages.

MMS: (MultimediaMmessages), introduced in iOS 3, MMS supports images, videos, sound, contact cards, and location data. Sent and received via the Messages app on iPhone to other mobile cell phones.

N

Newsstand: A special folder in iOS 5 that collects together magazine and newspaper apps and allows the automatic downloading of new issues.

Notification Center: A pull-down list of recent notifications, accessible from any iOS Home Screen or from within any iOS app.

P

Photos: Built-in Apple app that handles your photo albums on your iPhone and iPod touch 4, and synced photos and videos for iPhone and all generations of iPad and iPod touch.

Photo Stream: Part of iCloud, Photo Stream stores your last thirty days or 1000 photos online and on your iOS devices, and all your photos on your Mac.

Q

QuickTime: Apple's 2D video and graphics player, used to play movies and other video on iOS.

R

Retina Display: 960x640, 326ppi display available on iPhone 4 and iPod touch 4.

S

Safari: Apple's web browser, both for Mac OS X and iOS (sometimes called Mobile Safari). Based on KHTML/WebKit renderer and the Nitro JavaScript engine.

SIM card: Subscriber Identity Module. The little card used in mobile phones that connects the phone to the network.

Siri: Apple's intelligent virtual assistant, which replaces VoiceControl on the iPhone 4S.

Sleep/Wake Button: Physical hardware button on top of the iPhone, iPod touch, and iPad. Used to power on, wake from sleep, put to sleep, and power down iOS devices.

SMS: (Short Message Service) Text messages sent from the Messages app on iPhone to other cellmobile phones.

T

Twitter: One of the most popular social networks built around a follower/following system rather than friends, with messages limited to 140 characters.

V

VPN: (Virtual Private Network) provides secure access over the Internet to private networks, such as the network at your company or school.

W

Wi-Fi: A trademark of the Wi-Fi Alliance, commonly used to refer to 802.11g (pre-2010 iOS devices) or 802.11n (post-2010 iOS devices) wireless networking.

XYZ

YouTube: Google's web-based streaming video service. Accessible from iPhone or iPod touch via the YouTube app, or iPad either online or via the YouTube app.